STORIES
OF
THE PROPHETS

SAYYED ABUL HASAN ALI NADWI

UK ISLAMIC ACADEMY

Published by

UK Islamic Academy
147 Mere Road
Highfields, Leicester
LE5 5GQ
United Kingdom

Website: www.ukiabooks.com
E-mail: info@ukiabooks.com

British Library Cataloguing in Publication Data
A catalogue record for this book is available from the British Library.

بِسْمِ اللهِ الرَّحْمٰنِ الرَّحِيمِ

Dedication

Dear Nephew (Muhammad al-Hasani),

I know that you, like other children of your age, have a keen interest in reading and listening to stories. What saddens me is that stories you read are only about animals – cats, dogs, lions, wolves, monkeys and bears. We your elders are to blame for this sad state of affairs, for these are the only stories available for you.

That is why I planned to write a series of story books in Arabic suitable for children of your age, dealing with the life and the work of the Prophets and Messengers. *Qiṣaṣ al-Nabīyeen* (Stories Of The Prophets), being the first part of the series, is presented here. It is my gift to you.

In this series of stories I have tried to write in a way that suits the interests of children. That is why I have repeated certain expressions and kept the story simple. I believe this may be the first book of its kind for children studying in religious institutions. In future titles in this series, you will read other interesting, clear and moving accounts of other Prophets of Allah. What happens in these stories is very special, because, unlike other stories, they are totally free of any lie or falsehood.

May Allah, through you, bring happiness and peace to your parents, to your uncle and to Islam and help to restore the glory of your ancestors the Muslims who came before you. (Ameen)

Ali al-Hasani

Contents

Islamic and Biblical Names

Ādam	Adam
Ayyūb	Job
Benyāmīn	Benjamin
Dā'ūd	David
Hajar	Hagar
Hārūn	Aaron
Hūd	
Ibrāhīm	Abraham
'Isā	Jesus
Ishāq	Isaac
Ismā'īl	Ishmael
al-Khaḍir	
Lūṭ	Lot
Maryam	Mary
Mūsā	Moses
Nūh	Noah
Ṣāliḥ	
Sārah	Sarah
Shu'ayb	
Sulaymān	Soloman
Yahyā	John
Ya'qūb	Jacob
Yūnus	Jonah
Yusha'	Josuah
Yūsuf	Joseph
Zakariyyā	Zachariah

Foreword

The Prophets were chosen by Allah to guide mankind to the Divine Path. They faced many difficulties and suffered severe hardships in their efforts to call their straying people to obey and worship Allah. This edition of *Stories of the Prophets* presents the lives of Allah's Prophets (peace and blessing be upon them). The stories were written by the renowned Islamic scholar Maulana Sayyed Abul Hasan Ali Nadwi. He is one of the greatest living authorities on Islam and his works are used as textbooks throughout the Arab and Muslim world.

This translation from a major Arabic work provides English-speaking Muslims with the benefits of Maulana Sayyed Abul Hasan's scholarship. The stories which have been drawn from the Holy Qur'an constantly reflect the author's depth of knowledge. They are written in a lively style with subtleties explained and descriptions vividly portrayed to provide the reader with a clear picture of each Prophet's mission.

Each story is a delight to read and should provide both adults and children with a fresh insight into the life of the men Allah chose to guide their communities. The story of the last Prophet has not been included in this edition as it deserves a book to itself. To ensure that young people receive all the guidance, knowledge and inspiration that *Stories of the Prophets* offers, a workbook is included.

My thanks are due to Sis. Aisha Bewley, Sis. Maryam Davies, Bro. Jamil Qureshi, my daughters Su'ād, Shifa' and my other children for their help in producing this book. May Allah accept this effort and make it a source of inspiration and guidance for all.

Leicester (England)   **Iqbal Ahmad Azami**
Shawwal 1410 A.H
May 1990

6

Introduction

I know Sayyed Abul Hasan Nadwi, the author of this book, both in person and through his writings. I find in him the heart and mind of a Muslim — he has spent his whole life in the service of Islam — in addition to his thorough knowledge and insight into Islam. This is my testimony which I affirm for Allah's sake in this introduction.

Though quite small, *Stories of the Prophets* is a major work and a substantial addition to the *opus* of Sayyed Abul Hasan and his distinguished contemporaries in the field of Islamic *Da'wah* (in the Indian subcontinent). Islam must be taught in its pristine purity not only to adults but also to Muslim children. They are in greater need of such food for thought which may instruct them in the message of Islam. For it will help them grow up with the taste of Islam in their souls, the radiance of faith in their hearts and joy in their spirits. Stories are the basic constituency that help orient and mature the supple minds of children. Yet, though meant for children, this book will, I believe, be invaluable to adults also. For many Muslim adults taught under the colonial and Christian missionary-dominated educational system have been deprived of the opportunity to know the Qur'anic stories, to value their profound meaning, their spiritual quality, and their effectiveness, which are to the fore in this book.

I have read many books for children including those about the Stories of the Prophets (peace be upon them).

7

Indeed, I have been closely associated with a series of books drawn from the Holy Qur'an. Nonetheless, I testify without reservation, that Abul Hasan's present book surpasses all such works. What accounts for its excellence is the inclusion, with elucidation, of subtle teachings of the Qur'an, of explanations that highlight and reinforce the Qur'anic message, through the author's apt comments interwoven into the telling of the story. These comments provide glimpses of the greatest religious truths and they easily and effectively enter into the hearts of children and adults alike.

May Allah bestow His choicest rewards on Sayyed Abul Hasan and grant him the strength to carry out more such works. May Allah guide through his writings the future generations of Muslims that are under the constant attack of storms of disbelief, whose paths are strewn with thorns, whom black darkness surrounds, and who so urgently need guidance, light, care and sincere counselling for their growth. Allah alone grants the strength to accomplish every good deed.

Sayyed Qutb

1. The Prophet Nuh

After Adam (peace and blessings be upon him)*

Allah blessed the descendants of Adam, his children and grandchildren, and they spread and multiplied. If Adam had come back and seen them all, and someone had said to him, 'These are your descendants, Adam,' he would have been astonished. He would have said, 'Glory be to Allah! These are all my children! These are all my descendants!'

Adam's descendants founded many villages. They built many houses. They ploughed the land, grew crops and lived in comfort and contentment. They followed the way of their ancestor, Adam. They worshipped only Allah and did not worship anything else besides Him.

They were one united community. Adam was the one father of all of them, and Allah was their One Lord.

Satan's envy

Satan had not bowed down to Adam when Allah had commanded him to do so. So he was driven out and damned for ever. But how could Satan and his descendants be content with this? Were not people still worshipping

---

*Muslims are required to invoke Allah's blessings and peace upon the Prophets whenever their name is mentioned.

Allah? Were not people still a single community with no differences? That could not be! Would Adam's descendants go to the Garden while Iblis and his descendants went to the Fire? That could not be! Should not he take revenge on the sons of Adam so that they would go to the Fire with him?

Satan's idea

But how could Satan do that when people were worshipping Allah? He decided to call them to worship idols so that they would go to the Fire and never get to the Garden. He knew that Allah forgives people all sins, if He so wills, except one. Allah never forgives people worshipping other things besides Him or as well as Him.

So Satan decided to call the people to associate other things with Allah so that they would never go to the Garden. But how could he persuade them?

If he went to the people and said to them, 'Worship idols. Do not worship Allah,' they would curse him and chase him off. They would say: 'Allah forbid! How can we associate other things with our Lord? How can we worship idols? You are a cursed satan! You are a foul satan!'

So Satan had to look for another way, a cleverer way, to get the people to do as he wanted.

Satan's trick

There had been men who feared Allah and worshipped Him night and day and who remembered Him often. They had loved Allah, so Allah had loved them and answered their prayers. People loved them and spoke of them with respect long after they had died and gone to Allah's mercy.

Satan was well aware of this. So he went to the people and mentioned those men. He said, 'What do you think of So-and-so and So-and-so and So-and-so?'

They said, 'Glory be to Allah! They were men of Allah and His friends. When those men prayed, He answered them. When they asked, He gave to them.'

Pictures of the righteous men

Satan asked, 'How great is your sorrow for them?' They replied, 'Very great indeed.'

He asked, 'How great is your longing for them?' They replied, 'Very great indeed!'

He asked, 'Why don't you look at them every day then?' They said, 'How can we do that when they are dead?' He said, 'Make pictures of them and look at them every morning.'

People liked Satan's idea and made such pictures and looked at them every day. Whenever they saw the pictures, they remembered how those holy men had lived.

From pictures to statues

In time, the people moved on from making pictures to making statues. They made many statues of the holy men and put them in their houses and their mosques.

They still worshipped Allah and did not associate anything with Him. They knew that these were only statues of holy men and that they could neither help nor hurt them nor provide for them. They showed them respect because they were reminders of the holy men.

As time passed, the number of statues increased. The people respected them more and more. They got used

11

to having them around and looked for blessings in them. Now whenever one of their holy men died, they would make a statue of him and name it after him.

From statues to idols ·

Sons saw their fathers looking for blessings through the statues and saw how much respect they had for them. They saw them kiss the statues, dress them and pray to Allah in their presence. They saw them lower their heads and bow down in their presence.

When the fathers passed away, the sons added to what their fathers had done. They began to prostrate themselves before them, to ask the statues for things and to sacrifice animals to them. In this way the statues were turned into idols.

People began to worship them as they had worshipped Allah before. They had a lot of these idols. One was Wadd. Another was Suwa'. This was Yaghuth. That was Ya'uq. Another was Nasr.

Allah's anger

Allah became very angry with the people. He cursed them. How could Allah not be angry with the people because of what they were doing? Was this what they were created for? Was this what they were given provision for?

They walked on Allah's earth, but rejected Allah! They ate Allah's provision, but associated others with Allah! How terrible a sin!

Allah was so angry with the people that He held back the rain and made things hard for them. Their harvests were small and few children were born to them.

But the people did not learn their lesson from that, they did not understand. They did not turn to Allah in repentance. They needed good counsel.

The messenger

Allah does not speak to each person individually or tell each one to do this or do that. The angels are a race just like mankind. It is possible to see them and hear what they say, if Allah wills. But the angels do not speak to each person individually either, or tell each one to do this or do that. Only Allah can choose the person who will receive His message to give to the people. Allah wanted to send a messenger to the people who could speak to them and counsel them. Allah chose to send the children of Adam a man from among themselves to speak to them and give them good counsel.

Man or angel?

Allah wanted this messenger to be a man and to be one of the people. That way they would recognize him and understand what he said.

If the messenger had been an angel, the people might say, 'What has he got to do with us? He is an angel and we are mortals! We eat and drink and we have wives and children. How can we worship Allah?' But if the messenger were a man, he could answer, 'I eat and drink; I have a wife and children. But I worship Allah. Why don't you worship Allah?'

If the messenger had been an angel, the people might say to him, 'You do not get hungry or thirsty. You

13

do not get ill or die. So you can worship Allah and remember Him always!' But if the messenger were a man, he could answer, 'I am just like you. I get hungry and thirsty. I get ill and will die. But I worship Allah and remember Him. So why don't you worship Allah? Why don't you remember Him?' In this way the people would not be able to make up excuses.

Nuh the Messenger

Allah chose to send Nuh to his people.

There were wealthy people and leaders among the children of Adam, but Allah alone knew who should carry His message and who could bear His trust.

Nuh was a pious and generous man; he was intelligent and forbearing, compassionate and sincere. He was truthful and trustworthy and known for giving good counsel. Allah revealed to Nuh, *'Warn your people before a painful punishment comes to them.'* (71: 1) So Nuh stood up among his people and told them, *'I am a faithful messenger to you.'* (26: 107)

What answer did his people give to him?

When Nuh began to say to his people, *'I am a faithful messenger to you,'* (26: 107) some of them answered back, 'When did this man become a Prophet? Yesterday he was one of us and today he says, "I am Allah's messenger to you"!'

Nuh's friends said, 'This man used to play with us when we were young and he sat with us every day. When did he become a Prophet? Was it during the day or the night?'

14

The rich and proud said, 'Couldn't Allah find anyone except him? Has everyone else died? Couldn't He find anyone except a poor man from among the common people?'

The ignorant ones said to each other: *'This is only a man like yourselves. If Allah had willed, He would have sent down angels. We have never heard of this among our fathers, the ancients.'* (23: 24)

Some of the people said that Nuh only wanted to become a leader, a man of power and position among them, by saying he was the messenger of Allah.

Nuh and his people

People had got used to thinking that worshipping idols was the truth and a sensible thing to do. They thought that anyone who did not worship idols was foolish. They would say, 'Our fathers worshipped idols, so why doesn't this man worship them?'

Nuh thought that their fathers were in the wrong and unwise and that Adam, who was the father of the fathers, did not worship idols. He worshipped Allah alone. Nuh thought that the people were in the wrong and foolish when they worshipped stones and did not worship Allah who had created them.

Nuh stood up among his people, saying in his loudest voice, *'O my people! Worship Allah! You have no god but Him. Truly I fear for you the punishment of a dreadful day.'*

The Council of his people said, 'We see that you are in clear error.'

He said, 'My people, there is no error in me. But I am a messenger from the Lord of all the worlds. I convey

15

to you the messages of my Lord and I give you good advice, for I know from Allah what you do not know.' (7: 59–62)

'The lowliest follow you'

Nuh tried hard to make his people abandon idols and worship Allah alone. But only a few of those people who worked with their hands and ate lawful food, lawfully earned, believed in him.

The rich were too proud of being rich to believe. Their pride kept them from listening to Nuh. Their property and children distracted them from thinking about the Next World. They would say, 'We are nobles and those people are lowly.' When Nuh called them to Allah, they answered, 'How should we believe you when the lowliest follow you?' (26: 11)

They asked Nuh to drive the poor away. Nuh refused and said, 'I cannot drive away the believers. My door is not a king's door. I am only a clear warner.' (26: 114–15)

Nuh knew that those poor people were sincere believers and that Allah would be angry if he drove them away. Against the anger of Allah, no-one would be able to help him. Nuh said, 'My people, who could deliver me from Allah if I drive them away?' (11: 30)

The argument of the rich

The rich said to the people: 'Listen to us. What Nuh is calling you to is not true. It is not good. Why? Because we are the first to sample every good thing. We have every sort of good food, every sort of beautiful clothes. We set the fashion and people follow us. We have seen that we do not want for any good thing, and nobody out-does us in anything in the city.'

They said about the poor people who had believed in Nuh: 'If there had been any good in this religion, it would have come to us before these paupers. *If it had been any good, they would not be before us in attaining it.*' (46: 11)

Nuh's call

Nuh went on calling his people and trying hard to counsel them.

He said, 'O my people! I am a clear warner to you, saying "Worship Allah and fear Him and obey me that He may forgive you your sins and defer you to a specified term. When Allah's term comes, it cannot be deferred, if you only knew."' (71: 2–4)

Allah kept the rain from them and was angry with them. Their harvests were small and they had few children. Nuh told them: 'My people! If you believe, Allah will be pleased with you and remove this punishment.'

Then, when Allah sent the rain to them and blessed their crops and children, Nuh called his people and said to them: 'Don't you recognize Allah? These are the signs of Allah all around you. Can't you see them? Can't you see the heavens and the earth? Can't you see the sun and the moon? Who created the heavens? Who placed the moon in them as a light and made the sun a lamp? He created you and laid the earth as a carpet for you.'

But the people of Nuh would not understand and would not believe. When Nuh called them to Allah, they put their fingers in their ears. Now, how can anyone who

17

does not hear a message understand it? How can anyone who does not want to hear, hear?

Nuh's prayer

Nuh stayed with his people for nine hundred and fifty years, calling them to Allah, but his people would not believe. They would not stop worshipping idols. They refused to return to Allah.

How long could Nuh wait? How long could he watch the earth and its people being ruined? How long could he put up with his people worshipping stones? How long could he watch them eat from Allah's provisions while they worshipped something else?

Why did Nuh not get angry? He was more patient than anyone else could have been! Nine hundred and fifty years: Glory be to Allah!

Then Allah revealed to Nuh, *'None of your people will believe except those who have already believed.'* (11: 36)

When Nuh called his people again, they said, *'Nuh! You have disputed with us and you have disputed often with us, so bring us what you promised us if you are speaking the truth.'* (11: 32)

Nuh became angry for Allah and despaired of those people. He said, 'O Allah, do not leave even one of the unbelievers on the earth!'

The ark

Allah answered Nuh's prayer and He decided what the fate of the unbelievers would be. All of them would be drowned in a great flood.

Allah wanted to save Nuh and the believers. He commanded Nuh to build a great ship, and Nuh began straightaway.

The unbelievers from his people saw him working busily and they mocked: 'What is this, Nuh? Since when have you become a carpenter? Didn't we tell you not to sit with the carpenters and ironsmiths and now you have really become a carpenter!

'Where is this ship going, Nuh? Everything about you is unbelievable! Is it going to sail in the sand or climb up the mountains? The sea is a long way from here. Will the *jinn* carry it or will oxen pull it?'

Nuh heard all that and was patient. He had heard worse things and had been patient. But sometimes he would say to them, *'If you mock us, we will mock you as you mock.'* (11: 38)

The flood

The promise of Allah came. We seek refuge with Allah!

It rained and rained until the sky was like a sieve which could not hold the water. Water poured down and gushed up and flowed in until it surrounded the people on every side.

Then Allah revealed to Nuh, 'Take with you those of your people and family who believe.'

Allah revealed to Nuh to take with him a pair of every animal and bird, a male and a female, because the flood would cover the earth. Neither man nor beast would be saved from it. Nuh did so. With him in the Ark were those of his people who believed in him and a pair of every bird and animal.

The Ark rode with them on waves like mountains. The people outside the Ark climbed onto every high place and every hill, fleeing from Allah's punishment.

But there is no refuge from Allah except in Him.

Nuh's son

Nuh had a son who was with the unbelievers. Nuh saw his son in the flood and said, *'My son, embark with us and do not be with the unbelievers.'*

He said, 'I will seek refuge on a mountain that will protect me from the water.'

Nuh said, 'Today there is no protector from Allah's command except for the one to whom He shows mercy.'

The waves came between them and Nuh's son was among the drowned. (11: 42–3)

Nuh was sad about his son. How could he not be sad about his own son? He wanted to save him from the Fire on the Day of Judgement since he was not able to save him from the water. The Fire is worse than the water. The punishment of the Next World is harsher.

Did not Allah promise that He would save his family? Yes! And Allah's promise is true. He wanted to speak to Allah on behalf of his son.

'He is not one of your family'

Nuh called on his Lord and said, 'My son is part of my family and Your promise is true. You are the most just of those that judge.' (11: 45)

But Allah does not look at people's family trees. He looks at their actions. Allah does not accept pleas on behalf of idol-worshippers. The idol-worshipper is not part of a

Prophet's family, even if he is his son. Allah made Nuh aware of that. He said, *'Nuh, he is not part of your family; he is of evil conduct. Do not ask of Me that about which you do not know. I warn you lest you be one of the ignorant.'* (11: 46)

Nuh became aware and turned to Allah, repentant. He said: *'My Lord, I take refuge with You lest I should ask of You something about which I have no knowledge. If you do not forgive me and show mercy to me, I will be among the losers.'* (11: 47)

After the flood

When what Allah willed had happened and the unbelievers were drowned, the rain stopped and the water sank away.

The unbelievers of the people of Nuh were destroyed. Neither the heavens nor the earth wept for them. *It was said, 'Away with the wrong-doing people!'* (11: 44)

The Ark stopped on Mount Judi. *It was said, 'Nuh, get down in peace.'* (11: 48)

Nuh and the people of the Ark got down and walked on the earth in peace. Allah blessed the descendants of Nuh and they spread in the land and filled the earth. There were communities among them and there were Prophets and kings among them.

Peace be upon Nuh among all beings!
Peace be upon Nuh among all the worlds! (37: 79)

2. The Prophet Hud

After Nuh

Allah blessed the descendants of Nuh and they spread over the earth. One community from them was called 'Ad.

They were strong men with bodies like iron. They conquered everyone, and no-one was able to conquer them. They did not fear anyone but were feared by everyone.

Allah blessed the 'Ad in everything. Their camels and sheep filled the hills and valleys. Their horses filled the streets and footpaths of their cities. Their children filled the houses.

When the sheep and camels of the 'Ad went out to pasture, they made a very beautiful sight. When the children went out in the morning to play, they also made a very beautiful sight.

The land of the 'Ad was a fertile green land full of gardens and springs.

The 'Ad's rejection

But the 'Ad were not grateful to Allah for all these blessings. They forgot the story of the flood which they had heard from their fathers and whose traces they saw in the land. They forgot why Allah had sent the flood against the community of Nuh.

They began to worship idols as the community of Nuh had done. They carved them out of stone with their own hands and then prostrated themselves before them and worshipped them. They asked them for what they needed, prayed to them and sacrificed to them. They were following in the footsteps of Nuh's community.

Their intelligence did not keep them from worshipping idols. Their cleverness in the things of this world did not guide them in religion.

The tyranny of the 'Ad

The strength of the 'Ad became a curse for them and for the people because they did not believe in Allah and did not believe in the Next World.

What was to stop them from acting unjustly, from being tyrants and wronging people? They did not think anyone was above them. They did not fear any reckoning or punishment.

They were no better than wild animals. The high and great among them would wrong the low, the strong among them would live off the weak.

When they were angry, they were like mad elephants who kill whatever they meet in their way. When they made war, they destroyed every living thing. When they entered a village, they laid waste to it and made its mighty people lowly.

The weak were terrified of their evil and fled from their injustice. Their strength was a curse for them and for others. That is what happens with any people who do not fear Allah and do not believe in the Next World.

The castles of the 'Ad

The 'Ad did nothing but eat and drink, play and amuse themselves. They competed with each other in building high castles and spacious houses. They wasted their wealth on water, clay and stones. Whenever they saw an empty place or some high ground, they built a tall castle on it.

They built houses as if they were going to live forever and never die. They built castles without any need for them while some of the people could not find anything to eat or drink. The poor among them could not find anywhere to live while the houses of the rich were empty. Anyone who saw them and saw their castles would know straightaway that they did not believe in the Next World.

Hud the messenger

Allah wanted to send a messenger to the 'Ad. Allah does not like His slaves to disbelieve; He does not like cruelty and corruption in the earth.

The 'Ad did not use their intelligence for anything except eating and drinking, playing, amusing themselves and building houses. Their intelligence was wasted because they did not use it on religion. They did not understand and so they worshipped stones.

Allah wanted to send the 'Ad a messenger from among themselves to guide them, someone they would know and whose words they would understand.

Hud was that Messenger. He was born into a noble family and grew up intelligent and virtuous.

Hud's call

Hud stood up among his people and said, *'Oh my*

people, worship Allah. You have no god except Him.'
(11: 50)

He said, 'O people, how can you worship stones and not worship the One who created you!

'O people, how can you worship stones today which you had carved for yourselves only yesterday? Allah created you and provided for you. He blessed you in your property, children, crops and cattle. He made you rulers after the people of Nuh and gave you physical strength.

'Part of what you owe for these blessings is to worship Allah and not to worship anything but Him.

'The dog to which you throw a bone does not leave you and will follow you like a shadow. Have you ever seen a dog freely leave his master and go to someone else? Have you ever seen any animal prostrate before an idol? Is man lower than an animal or higher than an animal?'

The people's answer

The 'Ad were busy eating, drinking, playing and amusing themselves. They were content with the life of this world.

They were distressed by what Hud said. They said to each other, 'What is Hud saying? What does he mean? We do not understand what he says.'

They decided, 'He is a fool or a madman.'

When Hud called them again, the nobles of his people said, *'We see that you are in a state of folly and think that you are a liar.'*

He said, 'My people, there is no folly in me. Rather, I am a messenger from the Lord of all the worlds. I convey to you the messages of my Lord and I am a faithful adviser to you.' (7: 66–8)

25

Hud's wisdom

Hud worked hard to counsel his people. He called them with wisdom and kind-heartedness: 'O my people, I was your brother and friend yesterday. Don't you know me? My brothers! Why do you fear me and flee from me? I will not make you any poorer at all.

'O my people, I do not ask you for any wealth. My wage falls only on Allah. (11: 29)

'O my people, what do you have to fear if you believe in Allah? Allah will not lessen your riches at all if you believe in Him. Allah will bless you in your provision and increase it.

'My people, why are you surprised at my message? Allah does not speak to each person individually, telling each one to do this and to do that. Allah sends to every people a man from among them to speak to them and advise them. *Do you wonder that a reminder from your Lord should come to you by means of a man from among you that he may warn you?'* (7: 69)

Hud's belief

The 'Ad could not think of an answer. So they said, 'Our gods are angry with you. You have been afflicted by a mental disease. A curse from the gods has struck you.'

Hud said, 'These idols are only stones. They cannot help or hurt anyone; they neither speak nor hear nor see. They do not possess good or evil, they have no power to bring harm or benefit for anyone.

'You yourselves do not possess any benefit or harm for me. I do not believe in your gods and I do not fear them. *I am quit of what you associate.* (11: 54) And I do not fear you either. *Try your guile on me, all together.*

26

Truly, I have put my trust in Allah, my Lord and your Lord. (11: 56)

'Everything is under His control. Not even a single leaf falls from a tree without His permission.'

The 'Ad's stubbornness

The 'Ad heard all that, but still they did not believe. Hud's wisdom and good advice were wasted on them. They said, 'Hud, you have no proof or evidence! Hud, we will not abandon our ancient gods because of your new talk. Should we leave the gods our fathers worshipped for something someone says? Never!

'Hud, you do not believe in our gods and you do not fear them. Well, we do not believe in your God and we do not fear His punishment. You are always talking about the punishment, so where is it, Hud? When will it come?'

Hud said, *'The knowledge is with Allah. I am a clear warner.'* (67: 26)

They said, 'We are waiting for that punishment and want to see it.'

Hud was astonished at their impudence; his heart filled with sadness at their foolishness.

The punishment

The 'Ad looked into the sky for the rain they needed. They looked every day. They looked at the sky and did not see a wisp of cloud. They yearned for rain.

One day, they saw a cloud coming toward them. They were very happy and shouted, 'This is a rain cloud! This is a rain cloud!' People danced for joy. They called out to each other: 'A rain cloud! A rain cloud!'

27

But Hud understood that the punishment had come. He told them, 'This is not a cloud of mercy. It is a wind containing a painful punishment.'

So it was. A fierce wind blew whose like the people had never seen before. The tempest blew and uprooted trees and destroyed houses. It carried up animals and flung them far away. The desert sands were blown into the air and blacked out everything. No-one could see anything.

Terror filled the people and they ran into their houses and bolted the doors. The children clung to their mothers. People clung to the walls. The children were weeping and the women shouting. They were praying and begging for help.

It was as if someone was saying, *'There is no protector today from Allah's command.'* (11: 43)

That went on for eight days and seven nights.

The people were struck down like palm-trees fallen to the ground. It was a terrible sight. The once proud people were now only dead bodies and the birds ate them. Their grand houses were now only ruins and owls lived in them.

Hud and the believers were saved by their belief. The 'Ad were destroyed because of their disbelief and rebellion.

The 'Ad rejected their Lord. So away with the 'Ad, the people of Hud! (11: 60)

3. The Prophet Salih

After the 'Ad

The people of Thamud were the heirs to the 'Ad as they were the heirs to the community of Nuh. The Thamud followed after the 'Ad as the 'Ad had followed after Nuh. The land of Thamud was also a beautiful green land of gardens with running rivers and springs.

The Thamud were the same as the 'Ad in their culture and crops and in the vast number of their gardens. They excelled the 'Ad in intelligence and skill. They carved beautiful and spacious houses out of the mountains, and produced wonderful paintings on the stones. They skilfully worked stone as others might use soft wax.

Visitors to their city saw great palaces like mountains, looking as if they had been built by the *jinn,* colourful flowers painted on the walls looking as fresh as if the spring had brought them out.

Allah poured out blessings both in the heavens and the earth for the Thamud. Heaven was generous to them with rain. The earth was generous to them with plants and flowers. The gardens were generous to them with fruits. Allah blessed them in provisions and livelihood.

The Thamud's disbelief

However, none of that moved the people of

Thamud to be grateful and worship the glory and greatness of Allah. It led them to reject Allah and to be unjust. They forgot Allah while they rejoiced in what they had been given. They would say: 'Who is stronger than us?' They lived as if they believed that death would never enter their palaces and gardens, that they would own and enjoy them forever.

They thought that death would find no way to reach them in their high mountains. They thought that Nuh's community had only been drowned because they had been in a valley and that the 'Ad had been destroyed because they lived on a plain. They believed that the people of Thamud were in a place safe from fear and death.

Idol worship

But the people of Thamud went still further in their thanklessness. From the stones they carved they made idols and worshipped them, just as the community of Nuh and of the 'Ad had done.

Allah had made them masters of stone, but in their ignorance they became the slaves of stones. Allah had raised them up and provided them with good things, but they lowered themselves and dishonoured mankind. *Allah does not wrong people at all, but people wrong themselves.* (10: 44)

What strange madness! The very stones they carved, and with their own hands; stones that could neither hear them nor answer them in any way! They abased themselves before bits of senseless, lifeless rock and fell down in prostration.

Do the strong worship the weak? Does the master prostrate to his slave? But they forgot Allah and forgot themselves. They refused to worship Allah, so Allah brought down their pride.

Salih, the messenger

Allah willed for the people of Thamud a messenger. He sent them a messenger as He had sent one to the community of Nuh and then to the 'Ad.

Allah does not like His slaves to reject Him. Allah does not like corruption in the earth.

There was a man among them whose name was Salih. He had been born in a noble house and grew up intelligent and virtuous. Indeed, he was such a noble and sensible youth that people would point him out and say: 'This is Salih! This is Salih!' People had great hopes for him and thought that one day he would be one of their noblest and wealthiest men. They thought that he would have a great castle and a beautiful garden.

His father thought that his son would obtain great wealth through his intelligence and would stand out among people. He thought that he would ride on a fine horse followed by servants. People would greet him and say, 'This is the son of So-and-so!' How happy he imagined he would be when he heard people saying that he was most fortunate in his son who had become so very rich!

But Allah willed otherwise. Allah wanted to honour Salih with prophethood and to send him to his people to bring them out of the darkness into the light. What honour is greater, what nobility is higher, than that?

Salih's call

Salih stood up among his people, saying in his

31

loudest voice, *'O my people, worship Allah. You have no god but Him.'* (11: 61)

The rich people were busy eating and drinking, playing and amusing themselves. They worshipped idols and thought that there was no other god.

They did not like Salih's call. The wealthy men of Thamud became angry and exclaimed, 'Who is this?'

The servants replied, 'This is Salih.'

They asked, 'What does he say?'

They said, 'He says: "Worship Allah. You have no god but Him." He says that Allah will raise you up after your death and repay you. He says: "I am Allah's messenger. He has sent me to my people."'

The rich people laughed and said, 'A pauper! Can this man be a messenger? He has neither palace nor garden. He has neither crops nor palm-trees. How can he be a messenger?'

The propaganda of the rich

The rich of Thamud saw that some of the people inclined towards Salih. They feared for their position of leadership and said, *'This is nothing but a mortal like yourselves, who eats what you eat and drinks what you drink. If you obey a mortal like yourselves, you will be losers. What, does he promise you that when you are dead and become dust and bones, that you will be brought forth? Away, away with what you are promised! There is nothing but the life of this world. We live and we die and we shall not be raised up.*

'He is only a mortal who has forged lies against Allah and we do not believe him.' (23: 33–8)

'Our opinion was wrong'

The people rejected Salih and did not believe him. When Salih warned them and told them not to worship idols, they said: 'Salih, you used to be such a noble and sensible youth. We thought that you would become one of our great men and nobles. We thought that you would be like So-and-so and So-and-so. You have turned out to be a nobody. Those who were the same age as you and not as intelligent as you have become famous and powerful. But you, Salih, you chose the path of poverty. We were wrong in our opinion of you. We are disappointed in our hopes for you.

'Your poor father! He did not receive any good from you. Your poor mother! Her efforts on you were wasted.'

Salih heard all of this and was sad for his people.

When Salih passed by them, they would say: 'May Allah show mercy to Salih's father. His son is wasted.'

Salih's advice

Salih kept on giving advice to his people and calling them to Allah with wisdom and kind-heartedness. He said: 'My brothers, do you think you will be here forever? Do you think that you will live in these houses forever? Do you think that you will remain in these gardens and by these rivers? That you will always eat from these crops and trees? That you will always carve houses out of these mountains? Never! That will never be!

'Why did your fathers die, my brothers? They too had palaces and they too had gardens and springs. They too used to carve houses out of the mountains. But none of that helped them. None of that protected them!

'The Angel of Death came to them and found a way to reach them. So you will also die and Allah will raise you up again and question you about these blessings.'

'I do not ask you for a wage'

Salih said, 'My brothers! Why do you run away from me? What do you fear? I will not lessen your wealth at all. I do not ask you for anything. I advise you and convey to you the messages of my Lord.

'I do not ask you for any wage for it. My wage falls only on Allah, the Lord of all the worlds. (26: 145)

'My brothers! Why don't you obey me when I am a faithful adviser to you? Why do you obey those who oppress people and consume their property, those who have given themselves up to easy living and corrupt the land, and who do not put things right?'

The people were dumbfounded and could think of no answer. Instead, they said, *'You are one of the sorcerers. You are only a mortal like us, so bring a sign if you are speaking the truth.'* (26: 153–4)

The camel of Allah

Salih asked, 'What sign do you want?'

They said, 'If you are speaking the truth, then bring out a pregnant camel from this mountain!'

They knew that camels are only born from camels and that a camel does not grow out of the ground nor is it produced from stone. They were sure that Salih would be unable to do it. Then they would win!

But Salih had great faith in his Lord. He knew that Allah had the power to do anything.

Salih called on his Lord. All that the people had asked for was done. A pregnant she-camel came out of the mountain and gave birth.

The people were confused and astonished. But only one of them believed.

The arrangement

Salih then said, 'This is the she-camel from Allah. It is the sign of Allah. You asked and He created it for you by His power. So respect this camel. *Do not touch her with evil lest you be seized by a near punishment.* (11: 64)

'This camel should be allowed to eat and drink in the land of Allah and to come and go freely. You do not need to provide it with drink or fodder, there is plenty.'

The camel was very large indeed and very unusual in form. The other camels were afraid of it. Whenever the camel came and drank, the other camels shied and ran away.

Salih saw that and said, 'This camel will come one day and your camels the next day. One day, this camel will drink and the next day your camels will drink.'

That is how the bounds were arranged between Salih and the people of Thamud regarding the camel. When it was the camel's turn, it went and drank. When it was the people's camels' turn, they went and drank. For a time these bounds were kept.

The Thamud's injustice

But the Thamud were proud and broke the agreement. They said, 'Why can't our camels drink every day?'

They were angry at this camel from which their camels shied away. Salih had warned them to be gentle with this camel. But they did not heed the warning. They asked one another, 'Who will get rid of this camel?'

A man stood up and said, 'I will!' Another stood up and said, 'I will!'

The two wretched men went and waited for the camel. When the she-camel came near, the first man brought her down with an arrow. The second man finished her off.

The punishment

When Salih learned that the she-camel had been killed, he was very sad indeed. He told the people, *'Enjoy yourselves in your homes for three days. That is a promise not to be denied.'* (11: 65)

In the city nine evil-minded men who spread evil and corruption in the land plotted together to get rid of Salih. They said: 'We will kill Salih and his family at night. We will not be seen. So, if we are questioned about it, we will say, "We don't know anything."'

But Allah protected Salih and his family.

On the third day, the punishment came to the Thamud. As they woke up in the morning there was a Shout accompanied by a great earthquake. Their hearts were broken by the Shout and their houses were destroyed by the earthquake. It was a terrible day for the Thamud. All the unbelieving people died and the city was destroyed.

Salih and the believers left that wretched city. What could they have done there if they had stayed?

As Salih left, he looked sadly at the remains of his people. Now they were only corpses. He said with great sadness: *'O my people! I conveyed the message of my Lord to you and I advised you sincerely. But you do not love sincere advisers.'* (7: 79)

Today, in the place where the Thamud dwelt, there are only empty castles and disused wells. There are only deserted villages.

When the Messenger of Allah, may Allah bless him and grant him peace, passed by the dwelling places of the Thamud on his way to Syria, he told his Companions, 'Do not enter the houses of those who wronged themselves unless you enter weeping, fearing that the like of what befell them might befall you.'

The Thamud rejected their Lord. So away with the Thamud! (11: 68)

4. The Prophet Ibrahim

The idol-seller

In a city, long, long ago, there lived a very famous man whose name was Azar. He was famous because he was a seller of idols.

In a huge building in the middle of the city, the people kept lots of idols and bowed down before them. Azar was no different. He also would bow down before these idols, and worship them.

Azar's son

Azar had a son called Ibrahim who was very intelligent. Ibrahim would see the people bowing down before the idols. He knew that the idols were made of stone and could not speak or hear.

He knew that the idols could neither help nor harm anything. He saw flies sit on them without being driven away and mice eat the food left for the idols without any trouble.

So Ibrahim would ask himself, 'Why do people worship the idols? Why do they ask the idols for things?'

Ibrahim's advice

Ibrahim would say to his father: 'Father, why do you worship these idols? Why do you bow down to them?

'Father, why do you ask these idols for things, when they can neither speak nor hear? They can neither help nor harm anything, so why do you put food and drink before them? Why, when they cannot eat or drink?'

Azar became angry and did not understand what all these questions meant.

Ibrahim tried to give his people the same advice, but they became angry and did not understand what he meant either.

Ibrahim said, 'I will smash the idols when the people are away. Then they will understand me.'

Ibrahim breaks the idols

When the day of their festival came, the people rejoiced and set out for the celebrations along with their children.

Ibrahim's father, ready to set out, asked Ibrahim: 'Why don't you come with us?'

Ibrahim replied: 'No, I am not feeling well.'

So, when Ibrahim was left alone at home, he went out to the huge building where the idols were kept, and spoke to the idols. He said: 'How is it that you don't speak? How is it that you don't hear? There is food and drink here. Why don't you eat? Why don't you drink?'

The idols were silent because they were stones which of course cannot speak.

Ibrahim said, *'What is stopping you from speaking?'* (37: 92) When the idols remained silent, Ibrahim became angry and grabbed an axe.

He hit the idols with the axe and smashed them all except one. He left the largest idol standing there and hung the axe round its neck.

'Who did this?'

The people came back and went into the building where the idols were kept. They were especially keen to bow down before the idols because it was the day of their big festival. They were amazed and dumbfounded, bitter and angry at what they saw.

'Who has done this to our gods!' they cried. Then some of them said: *'We heard a young man called Ibrahim talking about them.'* (21: 59–60)

When Ibrahim was brought to them, they said, *'Are you the one who did this to our gods?'* (21: 62)

Ibrahim, pointing to the largest idol, answered calmly: *'But this, their chief has done it. Question them if they are able to speak.'* (21: 63)

The people knew that the idols were made of stone and that stones cannot hear or speak. They knew that the largest idol was made of stone and that it could not move, so it could not have broken the other idols.

They said to Ibrahim, 'You know that idols cannot speak.' And so he asked them: 'So how can you worship idols when they can neither help nor harm anything? Don't you understand anything? Don't you have any sense at all?'

The people were as silent as the idols, and ashamed.

A cool fire

The people met and said, 'What shall we do? Ibrahim has broken the idols and humiliated the gods. How should we punish him? How should we pay him back for what he has done?'

The answer was, *'Burn him and stand by your gods.'* (21: 68)

That is what they did. They lit a fire and threw Ibrahim into it.

But Allah helped Ibrahim and said to the fire, *'Fire, be coolness and safety to Ibrahim.'* (21: 68)

And so it was. The fire was coolness and safety for Ibrahim. The people saw that the fire did not hurt Ibrahim and they saw that he was not harmed by the smoke and the flames.

Once again, they were amazed and confused.

'Who is my Lord?'

That night Ibrahim saw a star and he said, 'This is my Lord.' When the star set, Ibrahim exclaimed, 'No! This is not my Lord!' Ibrahim saw the moon and he said, 'This is my Lord.' When the moon set, Ibrahim exclaimed, 'No! This is not my Lord!' The sun rose and Ibrahim said, *'This is my Lord. This is greater.'* (6: 78) When the sun set, Ibrahim exclaimed, 'No! This is not my Lord! Allah is my Lord, He is always living and does not die. The light of Allah shines always and never dims and never sets. Allah is All-Mighty, nothing can overcome Him. The light of the stars is weak, morning overcomes it. The light of the moon is weak, the sun overcomes it. The light of the sun is weak, night overcomes it and clouds overcome it. Stars cannot help me because they are weak. The moon cannot help me because it is weak. The sun cannot help me because it is weak. Allah alone can help me.'

'My Lord is Allah'

Ibrahim knew that Allah was his Lord, for Allah is always living and does not die; His light shines always and never dims nor sets. Allah is All-Mighty, nothing can overcome Him.

Ibrahim knew that Allah is the Lord of the stars, and the Lord of the moon, and the Lord of the sun, and the Lord of all the worlds that may be.

Thus Allah guided Ibrahim and made him a Prophet and His close friend. Allah commanded Ibrahim to call his people and tell them not to worship idols.

Ibrahim's call

Ibrahim carried out the command of his Lord. He asked his people: 'What do you worship?'

'We worship idols,' (26: 71) they said.

Ibrahim asked them: *'Do they hear you when you call? Or help or harm you?'*

They said, 'We found our fathers doing that.' (26: 72–4)

Ibrahim said: 'I do not worship these idols. Rather, I am the enemy of these idols. I worship the Lord of all the worlds, *the One who created me and who guides me, the One who gives me food and drink, the One who heals me when I am ill, and the One who makes me die and brings me to life.* (26: 78–81)

'But idols do not create and do not guide. They do not give anyone food or drink. When someone is ill, they do not heal him. They do not make anyone die nor bring anyone to life.'

Before the King

A great king ruled that city, and he ruled like a cruel tyrant. People had to bow down before him. When the

King heard that Ibrahim prostrated himself only before Allah and would not prostrate himself before anyone else, he became angry and sent for him. Ibrahim came straightaway: he did not fear anyone except Allah.

The King asked: 'Who is your Lord, Ibrahim?'

Ibrahim said: 'My Lord is Allah.'

The King asked: 'Who is Allah, Ibrahim?'

Ibrahim said: *The One Who gives life and death.'* (2: 258)

The King said: *'I give life and death.'* (2: 258) Then he had a man brought before him and had him killed. Then he had another man brought before him and let him live. After that, very proudly, he said: 'You see! I give life and death. I killed one man and let the other man live.'

The King was very silly. All idol-worshippers are foolish in such matters. Ibrahim wanted to make the King understand. He wanted to make all his people understand.

He said to the King: 'Allah brings the sun from the east. Now you bring it from the west.'

The King was confused and silent. He was ashamed and could think of nothing to say.

Calling his father to Allah

Ibrahim also wanted to call his father to Allah. He said to him: 'O my father, why do you worship something that does not hear or see? Why do you worship something that cannot help or harm anyone? *My father, do not worship Satan!* (19: 44) Worship the Merciful!'

Ibrahim's father became angry and said, 'I will beat you. Leave me alone. Do not talk to me.'

Ibrahim was patient. He said to his father, 'Peace be upon you. I will leave this place and call on my Lord.'

43

Ibrahim was very sad. He wanted to go to another country only so that he could worship his Lord and call people to Allah in peace.

To Makka

Ibrahim's people had become angry. The King had become angry. Even Ibrahim's father had become angry.

Ibrahim decided to travel to a different land where he could worship Allah and call people to Allah in peace. He said good-bye to his father and left his land.

Ibrahim made for Makka with his wife Hajar. There were no plants or trees in Makka, no well or river, and no animals or people.

Ibrahim reached Makka and stayed there for a time. After that, he left his wife Hajar and his son Isma'il. When he was about to leave, his wife asked: 'Where are you going? Are you going to leave us here? Are you going to leave us here when there is no food nor water? Has Allah commanded you to do this?'

Ibrahim said, 'Yes.'

Hajar said, 'Then He will not let us die.'

The well of Zamzam

Isma'il became thirsty and his mother wanted to give him some water. But where was there any water? There was no well in Makka! There was no river in Makka! Hajar looked for water; she ran from Safa to Marwa and from Marwa to Safa.

Allah helped Hajar and Isma'il. He created water for them. Water sprang out of the ground and Isma'il and Hajar drank from it. The water remained there and became known as the well of Zamzam. Allah has blessed the water of Zamzam. This is the well from which people drink during the *Hajj*. They take the Zamzam water back to their own countries to share with their families and friends. Have you drunk Zamzam water?

Ibrahim's dream

Some time later Ibrahim returned to Makka and rejoined Isma'il and Hajar. Ibrahim was very happy with his young son Isma'il. He ran and played and went about with his father who loved Isma'il deeply.

One night Ibrahim had a dream. He dreamt that he sacrificed Isma'il.

Ibrahim was a truthful Prophet. His dream was a true dream. Ibrahim was a close friend of Allah and he decided to do what Allah had commanded him to do in the dream. But first he asked of Isma'il: *'I have seen in a dream that I must sacrifice you. So what do you think?'*

He said, 'My father, do what you are commanded. Allah willing, you will find me one of the steadfast.' (37: 102)

Ibrahim took Isma'il with him, and a knife.

When Ibrahim reached Mina, he made ready to sacrifice Isma'il. Isma'il lay down on the ground and Ibrahim was about to sacrifice him. He put the knife against Isma'il's throat. Allah wanted to see if His friend would do what he was commanded to do. Did he love Allah more or did he love his son more?

When Ibrahim had passed the test, Allah sent Jibril with a ram from the Garden. He said: 'Sacrifice this ram. Do not sacrifice Isma'il.'

Allah liked what Ibrahim had done. So He commanded the Muslims to make a sacrifice in remembrance on the 'Id al-Adha.

May Allah bless Ibrahim, the close friend of Allah and grant him peace.

The Ka'ba

Ibrahim left Makka a second time and returned a second time. He decided to build a house for Allah. There were many houses, but there was no house for Allah where He alone was worshipped.

Isma'il wanted to help build this house for Allah. So father and son both worked, carrying stones from the mountains around Makka, and built the Ka'ba with their own hands.

Ibrahim would always remember Allah and call on Him. He said: *'Our Lord, accept this from us! You are the All-Hearing, the All-Seeing!'* (2: 127)

Allah accepted it from Ibrahim and Isma'il, and blessed the Ka'ba.

We Muslims face the Ka'ba in every prayer. We travel to the Ka'ba during the *Hajj,* and go around it in *tawaf* and pray there.

May Allah bless Ibrahim and grant him peace! May Allah bless Isma'il and grant him peace! May Allah bless Muhammad and grant him peace!

Jerusalem

Ibrahim had another wife whose name was Sarah.

By Sarah, Ibrahim had another son whose name was Ishaq. Ibrahim and Ishaq lived in Palestine. Ishaq built a house for Allah in Palestine just as his father and brother had built a house for Allah in Makka.

This mosque which Ishaq built in Palestine is in

Jerusalem. It is the Al-Aqsa Mosque and Allah blessed the land around it.

Allah blessed the sons of Ishaq as He blessed the sons of Isma'il. There were Prophets and kings among them. Ishaq had a son whose name was Ya'qub. He was a Prophet. Ya'qub had twelve sons, including Yusuf ibn Ya'qub. The wonderful story of Yusuf is in the Qur'an. Here is that story.

5. The Prophet Yusuf

A wonderful dream

Yusuf was a young boy, both handsome and intelligent. He had eleven brothers. His father Ya'qub loved him more than any of his other sons.

One night Yusuf had a wonderful dream. He saw eleven stars and the sun and the moon all bowing down to him. He was quite amazed by the dream. What did it mean? How could the stars, the sun and the moon bow down to a man? Young Yusuf went to his father Ya'qub and told him about his dream.

He said, *'Father, I saw eleven stars, the sun and the moon in a dream. I saw them bowing down to me.'* (12:4)

Ya'qub was a Prophet and understood. He was very happy about this dream. He said, 'Allah has blessed you, Yusuf. Something great will happen to you. This dream contains the good news that you will be given knowledge and prophecy. Allah blessed your grandfather, Ishaq, and He blessed your ancestor, Ibrahim. He will bless you and He will bless the family of Ya'qub.'

Ya'qub was an old man who knew about human nature. He knew how Satan can confuse and overcome people.

He said: 'My son, do not tell any of your brothers about your dream. They will envy you and become your enemies.'

The brothers' envy

Yusuf had another brother by the same mother. His name was Benyamin. Ya'qub loved them both very much. He did not love anyone as much as he loved them.

The brothers were jealous of Yusuf and Benyamin and were very bitter. They would say: 'Why does our father love Yusuf and Benyamin more than us? Why does he love them when they are young and weak? Why doesn't he love us as much, when we are strong young men? This is very strange indeed.'

Yusuf was young and innocent. He told his brothers about his dream. The brothers got very angry indeed when they heard about it, and became even more jealous.

One day the brothers got together and said: 'If we kill Yusuf or drive him away to some distant land, then we will have our father's love all to ourselves and he will love only us.'

One of them said: 'No! Throw him into a well beside the road. Then some travellers will take him.'

Finally, the brothers agreed to that plan.

A delegation to Ya'qub

Then, the ten brothers went to Ya'qub. Ya'qub was very afraid for Yusuf. He knew that the brothers were jealous of him and did not love him, so he would not allow Yusuf to go away with them. Yusuf used to play with his brother Benyamin but he did not go far away. The brothers knew this, but they had decided to do something wicked.

They said: 'Father, why won't you allow Yusuf to come with us? What are you afraid of? He is our dear, little brother. We are the sons of the same father. Brothers always play together, so why don't we? *Send him with us tomorrow to frolic and play. We will watch over him.'* (12: 12)

Ya'qub was an old man, intelligent and wise, and patient. He did not want Yusuf to go far away from him because he was very much afraid for him. He told his sons, *'I fear that the wolf may eat him while you are neglecting him.'* (12: 13)

They said, 'Never! How can the wolf eat him while we are there? How could it eat him when we are strong young men?'

In the end Ya'qub gave Yusuf permission to go with his brothers.

To the wilderness

The brothers were very happy when Ya'qub gave Yusuf permission to go with them. They took Yusuf into the wilderness and threw him into a well there. They showed no mercy to little Yusuf. They showed no mercy to their father Ya'qub either.

Yusuf was all alone in the deep, dark well. But Allah told him: 'Do not be sad. Do not be afraid. Allah is with you. Something great will happen to you. Your brothers will come before you and you will tell them what they did.'

After the brothers had thrown Yusuf into the well, they got together and said: 'What shall we tell our father?'

One of them said: 'Our father said, "I fear that a wolf may eat him." We will tell him, "You were right, father, a wolf did eat him."' The brothers agreed: 'Yes, we will tell him, "Father, the wolf ate him."'

One of the brothers then asked: 'But what proof will we have for that?' The others answered: 'Blood will provide evidence.'

The brothers caught a ram and killed it. Then they took Yusuf's shirt and dipped it in the blood. They were very pleased with themselves. They said: 'Now our father will believe us.'

Before Ya'qub

They came weeping to their father in the evening. They said: 'Father, we went running races and left Yusuf with our bags and the wolf ate him.' (12: 17)

They brought his shirt with false blood on it. (12: 18) They said: 'This is Yusuf's blood.'

Their father Ya'qub was a Prophet and an old man, much wiser than his sons. Ya'qub knew that when a wolf eats someone, it rips his clothes.

Yusuf's shirt was whole, it had only been dipped in blood. So Ya'qub knew that it was not Yusuf's blood and that the story about the wolf had been made up. He told his sons: 'This is a story that you have made up. Patience is good.' (12: 18) Ya'qub was sad indeed about Yusuf, but he had plenty of patience.

Yusuf in the well

The brothers had returned home, leaving Yusuf in the well. They had eaten and now slept in their beds. Yusuf, all alone in the well had neither slept nor eaten. The brothers forgot about Yusuf. But Yusuf did not sleep and he did not forget anyone.

Ya'qub kept thinking about Yusuf and Yusuf kept thinking about Ya'qub. It was a terrible time for Yusuf in that deep well, out in the wilderness, hidden far down in darkness.

51

From the well to the palace

A group of people were travelling to Egypt through that wilderness. They were thirsty and looking for water. They saw the well and sent a man to it to bring them some water.

The man came to the well and let down the bucket. He pulled the bucket up and there was a boy in it! Surprised, the man called out: *'Good news! Here is a boy!'* (12: 18)

The people hid Yusuf among their merchandise until they had travelled out of the area. When they got to Egypt, they stood in the market shouting: 'Who will buy this boy? Who will buy this boy?'

The Aziz* of Egypt bought Yusuf for a few silver coins. The merchants who sold him did not recognize the worth of Yusuf. The Aziz took him to his palace and told his wife: 'Treat Yusuf well. He is an intelligent boy.'

Faithfulness and trustworthiness

The wife of the Aziz was attracted to Yusuf. But Yusuf refused her advances and said: 'No! I will not break my master's trust. He has been good to me and he has treated me well. I fear Allah.'

The wife of the Aziz became angry and complained to her husband, but he knew that she was lying. He knew that Yusuf was trustworthy. He told his wife: *'You are one of those who are in error.'* (12: 29)

Yusuf was well-known in Egypt for his good looks. When anyone saw him, they would say, *'This is no mortal! He can only be a noble angel!'* (12: 31)

---

*'Aziz' signified a mighty person, a king etc., and was the title given to those who ruled Misr and Alexandria.

The wife of the Aziz became very angry indeed when Yusuf kept refusing her and she said to him: 'Then you will go to prison!'

Yusuf said, *'I prefer prison.'* (12: 33)

A few days later, the Aziz decided it was better to send Yusuf to prison. He knew that Yusuf was innocent, but even so Yusuf went to prison.

The warning in the prison

The people in the prison knew that Yusuf was a noble young man with great knowledge and a merciful heart. They loved and respected him.

Two other prisoners told Yusuf about their dreams. *One of them said: 'I dreamed that I was pressing grapes.' The other said: 'I dreamed that I was carrying bread on my head and the birds were eating from it.'* (12: 36)

They asked Yusuf to tell them the meaning of their dreams. Yusuf knew the meaning of dreams since he was a Prophet.

In Yusuf's time, people worshipped things other than Allah. They said: 'This is the lord of the earth. This is the lord of the sea. This is the lord of crops. This is the lord of rain.'

Yusuf would hear all that nonsense and weep for the ignorance of the people. He wanted to call people to the worship of Allah.

Allah wanted that to happen also in the prison. Did not the people in prison deserve to be warned? Did not they deserve mercy too? Are not the people in prison slaves of Allah, are not they too sons of Adam?

Even in prison Yusuf was free and brave in spirit. He was poor but generous and open-hearted. The Prophets proclaim the truth everywhere because the truth is a blessing, and the Prophets are generous with blessings in every time and place.

Yusuf's wisdom

Yusuf said to himself: 'Need has driven these two men to me. The person who is in need is more open and humble. The person who is in need hears and obeys. If I teach these men something now, they will listen, and the people of the prison will also listen.'

So Yusuf did not rush to answer their questions. He said: *'I will tell you its interpretation before your food is brought to you.'* (12: 37)

The two men sat down and were calm. Then Yusuf said to them: 'I know how to interpret dreams. *That is part of what my Lord has taught me.'*

The men were content to wait and listened patiently. Yusuf began his warning.

The warning of *tawhid*

Yusuf said: *'That is part of what my Lord has taught me.* But Allah does not give His knowledge to everyone. Allah does not give His knowledge to an idol-worshipper. Do you know why my Lord has taught me? Because I have left the path of idol-worship *and I have followed the religion of my fathers, Ibrahim, Ishaq and Ya'qub. It is not proper for us to associate anything with Allah.'*

Yusuf said: 'This *tawhid* does not belong only to us. It is for all people. *That is part of Allah's bounty to us and to mankind, but most people are not thankful.'* (12: 38)

Here Yusuf stopped and asked them: 'You say: "The

Lord of the earth and the Lord of the sea and the Lord of crops and the Lord of rain." We say: "Allah, the Lord of the Universe."

'Which is better, many different gods or Allah, the One, the All-Powerful? (12: 39)

'Where is the Lord of the earth, the Lord of the sea, the Lord of crops and the Lord of the rain? *Show me what they have created in the earth or do they have any share in the heavens?*

'Look at the earth and at the heaven. Look at man. *This is the creation of Allah. Show me what these others have created.*

'How can there be a Lord of the earth, a Lord of the sea, a Lord of crops and a Lord of the rain? *They are only names you yourselves have named, you and your fathers.*

'Judgement belongs to Allah. The Kingdom belongs to Allah. *The earth belongs to Allah. The command belongs to Allah.*

'Worship Him alone.

'That is the right religion, but most people do not know.' (12: 40)

The meaning of the dreams

When Yusuf finished warning them, he told them the meaning of their dreams. He said, *'As for one of you, he will pour wine for his lord. As for the other, he will be crucified and the birds will eat from his head.'* (12: 41) Then he said to the first man: *'Mention me in the presence of your lord.'* (12: 42)

The two men left. The first became a wine-bearer to the King. The other man was crucified. The wine-bearer

55

forgot to mention Yusuf in the presence of the King, so Yusuf remained in prison for several years.

The King's dream

The King of Egypt had a strange dream. He saw in the dream seven fat cows eaten up by seven thin cows. The King also saw seven green ears of corn, then seven withered ears.

The King was puzzled by this strange dream and asked his companions what it meant. But they only said: 'It is nothing. When someone is asleep, he sees many things which are not real.'

But the wine-bearer said: 'Not so. I will tell you the meaning of this dream.'

The wine-bearer then went to the prison and asked Yusuf the meaning of the King's dream. Yusuf was noble and generous, kind and understanding to Allah's creatures. He not only explained the meaning of the dream, he also explained what should be done about it. He said: 'You should plant your crops for seven years and leave the grain you harvest in the ear except for a little which you eat. After that will come a drought of seven years. After that help will come and the people will have plenty.'

The wine-bearer went to the King and told him the meaning of his dream.

The King sends for Yusuf

When the King heard all that, he was very relieved and happy. He asked: 'Who told you the meaning of the dream? Who is this noble man who has given us this advice and shown us what to do?'

The wine-bearer said: 'It is Yusuf the truthful. He is the one who told me that I would be a wine-bearer to my master, the King.'

The King wanted to meet Yusuf and sent for him. He said: *'Bring him to me! I would attach him to myself.'* (12: 54)

Yusuf asks for an inquiry into his case

The messenger came to Yusuf and gave him the King's summons. But Yusuf was not ready to leave prison in that way. People would say: 'This is Yusuf! He was in prison only the other day. He was unfaithful to the Aziz.'

Yusuf was proud and firm, intelligent and wise. Not many people in his place could have been so. If they had been, as Yusuf was, in prison for many years, and then a messenger from the King had come to them and said: 'The King has summoned you and is waiting for you,' they would have rushed to leave the prison.

But Yusuf told the King's messenger: 'Before I leave prison I want an inquiry into my case.'

The King ordered an investigation into Yusuf's case and this proved that Yusuf was innocent. So Yusuf left prison an innocent man. The King received him with honour.

Yusuf the ruler in charge of Egypt's grain storehouses

Yusuf knew that some people were not trustworthy, that they cheated a lot. In Egypt there were many storehouses for grain, but there was no grain in them. They were empty because the people who ran them were not trustworthy, they did not fear Allah. Their dogs would eat while the common people had nothing. Their houses would be smartly decorated while the common people had nothing to wear.

The common people could never benefit from Egypt's grain storehouses unless a guardian with knowledge was put in charge of them. A guardian without knowledge would not know how to run them wisely. Someone who had knowledge but was not an honest guardian would cheat the people and use the storehouses for his own benefit.

Yusuf was an honest man and he had knowledge. He did not want to see the authorities ignoring the people's rights any more. He could not bear to see people starve.

Yusuf was not ashamed of the truth. He told the King: *'Set me over the treasuries of the land. I am a knowing guardian.'* (12: 55)

That is how Yusuf was put in charge of the grain storehouses of Egypt. The common people were very relieved and praised Allah.

Yusuf's brothers come

Just as Yusuf had foretold, there was indeed a famine in Egypt and Palestine. The people of Palestine heard that there was a merciful man in Egypt, a generous and noble man, in charge of the storehouses of the land, someone to whom people could go and get food. So Ya'qub sent his older sons to Egypt with money to buy food.

Benyamin stayed with his father because Ya'qub loved him very much. He did not want to be far from him. Ya'qub was afraid for him as he had been afraid for Yusuf.

Yusuf's brothers set out to meet the noble man of Egypt, not knowing that he was their own brother, Yusuf.

58

They thought that Yusuf was dead. How could he not be dead when they had thrown him into that deep, dark well, way out in the wilderness.

Yusuf's brothers came and went to him. He knew them, but they did not know him. (12: 58)

Yusuf remembered how they had thrown him into the well, how they had wanted to kill him. But Allah had saved him. Yusuf did not say anything to them. He did not disgrace them.

Yusuf and his brothers

Yusuf spoke to the brothers for a time and then asked: 'Where are you from?'

'From Canaan,' they replied.

He asked: 'Who is your father?'

'Ya'qub, son of Ishaq, son of Ibrahim, peace and blessings be upon them.'

He asked, 'Do you have another brother?'

'Yes,' they replied. 'We have a brother whose name is Benyamin.'

He asked: 'Why didn't he come with you?'

'Because,' they explained, 'our father would not let him. He does not like him to be far from him.'

Yusuf asked: 'Why won't he let him go? Is he a very young child?'

'No, but he had a brother named Yusuf. He once went with us and we went to run races and left Yusuf with our bags. A wolf ate him.'

Yusuf laughed to himself, but he did not say anything. He longed to see his brother Benyamin.

Allah had prepared another test for Ya'qub, the father of all the brothers.

Yusuf ordered that they be given food. Then he told them, *'Bring me your brother from your father.* (12: 59) If you do not bring him, you will not get any more food.'

Then Yusuf had their money secretly put back in their bags.

Ya'qub and his sons

The ten brothers went back to their father and told him the news. They said to him: 'Send our brother Benyamin with us. If you don't, we will not get any more food from the Aziz.' They told Ya'qub, *'We will watch over him.'* (12: 63)

Ya'qub said: *'Shall I entrust him to you other than the way I entrusted to you before?* (12: 64) Have you forgotten the story of Yusuf? Will you watch over Benyamin the way you watched over Yusuf? *Allah is the best watcher. He is the most Merciful of the Merciful.'* (12: 64)

The brothers then found their money in their bags and told their father: 'The Aziz is a generous man. He has given us our money back. He did not charge us anything! Send Benyamin with us and we will also get his share.'

Ya'qub told them: 'I will not send him with you until you make a pledge by Allah that you will bring him back unless you are overcome.'

They made a pledge by Allah. Ya'qub said: *'Allah is the Guardian over what we say.'* (12: 66)

Then Ya'qub advised them: *'My sons, do not enter by the same gate. Enter by separate gates.'* (12: 67)

Yusuf meets his brother Benyamin

When the brothers returned to Egypt to buy more

food, they entered by separate gates as their father had told them to do.

When Yusuf saw Benyamin, he was very happy and had him stay in his house. Yusuf said to Benyamin: *'I am your brother.'* (12: 69) Benyamin was very happy to meet his brother who he believed had died many years before. Yusuf remembered his mother and father, his home; his childhood returned to him in awakened memories.

Yusuf wanted Benyamin to stay with him so that he could see him and speak to him every day and ask him about his home. But how could he make that happen when Benyamin was going back to Canaan the next day, when the brothers had made a pledge by Allah that they would take him back with them? How could Yusuf keep Benyamin with him for no reason? People would say, 'The Aziz has detained a Canaanite for no reason. This is a great injustice.'

But Yusuf was intelligent and clever.

He had a precious drinking cup placed secretly inside Benyamin's bags. Then, when the brothers left the next day, some of Yusuf's people went after them. Yusuf himself followed a little later. When they caught up with the brothers, they proclaimed: 'You are thieves!'

The brothers were surprised and asked: 'What are you missing?'

They said: 'We are missing the King's cup. Whoever brings it will have a camel's load in return.' (12: 72)

The brothers said: *'By Allah, you know that we have not come to make trouble in the land. We are not thieves.'* (12: 73)

They said: *'What will its repayment be if you are liars?'* (12: 73–4)

The brothers said: *'Its repayment will be the person in whose saddle-bag it is found. That is how we repay wrongdoers.'* (12: 75)

The cup was found in Benyamin's saddle-bag. The brothers were ashamed, but they were without shame when they said: 'If Benyamin stole, a brother of his stole before.' Yusuf, who had now reached the others, heard this lie, but he was silent and did not get angry. He was noble and patient. The brothers appealed to him.

They said: 'O Aziz! He has an aged father who is very old. Take one of us in his place. We see that you are one of those who do good.'

He said: 'Allah forbid that we should take anyone except the one in whose possession we found our goods. If we did so, we would be wrongdoers.' (12: 78–9)

So Benyamin stayed behind with Yusuf. The two brothers were happy. Yusuf had been alone for a very long time without seeing any of his family. Allah had sent Benyamin to him. So why should not he keep his brother with him so that he could see him and talk to him?

To Ya'qub

The brothers were confused. How could they go back to their father without Benyamin? The brothers thought about what they could tell their father. They had made him suffer over Yusuf. Could they now make him suffer over Benyamin?

The oldest of them refused to go back to Ya'qub. He told his brothers: *'Go back to your father and say, "Father, your son stole. We only testify to what we know. We are not guardians of the Unseen."'* (12: 81)

When Ya'qub heard their story, he knew that Allah

62

had had a hand in it, and he understood that Allah was testing him. He had been made to suffer over Yusuf before, now he was made to suffer over Benyamin. Allah would not impose two afflictions on him. Allah would not make him suffer over both Yusuf and Benyamin.

Allah had a hidden hand, and a hidden wisdom, in it. In such ways He tests his slaves and then He makes them happy and blesses them.

Also, the oldest son had stayed behind in Egypt, refusing to return to Canaan. Would Ya'qub be made to suffer over a third son when he had already been made to suffer over two sons? It could not be so!

Finally, when Ya'qub was calm again, he said: *'Perhaps Allah will bring them all to me. Allah is the All-Knowing, the All-Wise.'* (12: 83)

The secret disclosed

Yet, Ya'qub was, after all, a human being, with a soft, human heart in his breast. He did not have a piece of stone there. So, when he remembered Yusuf, his sorrow came flooding back again. He said: *'O my sorrow for Yusuf!'* (12: 84)

His sons were annoyed and said: 'You will keep on mentioning Yusuf until you die.'

Ya'qub said: *'I complain of my grief and sorrow to Allah. I know from Allah what you do not know.'* (12: 86)

Ya'qub knew that despair is disbelief. He had great hope in Allah. He sent his sons back to Egypt to look for Benyamin and Yusuf and to try hard to bring them home. Ya'qub forbade them to lose hope in Allah's mercy.

The brothers arrived in Egypt for the third time. They went to Yusuf and complained to him about their poverty and affliction. They asked him to be charitable to them.

Sorrow and love rose up in Yusuf. He could no longer bear to listen to the sons of his own father, the sons of Prophets, complaining about their poverty and affliction to one of the kings! He thought: How long can I conceal the truth from them when they are in need? How long can I go without seeing my father? Then, he said to them: *'Do you know what you did to Yusuf and his brother when you were ignorant?'* (12: 89)

The brothers knew that this was a secret known only to themselves and to Yusuf, so they knew that this Aziz was Yusuf.

Glory be to Allah! Could Yusuf be alive? He had not died in the well! Could Yusuf be the Aziz of Egypt, the famous man in charge of the storehouses of the land, the one who provided food for them?

They had no doubt that the one who had spoken to them was Yusuf, son of Ya'qub. *They said: 'You are Yusuf.'* (12: 90)

He answered: *'I am Yusuf and this Benyamin is my brother. Allah has been good to us. Whoever fears Allah and is patient, Allah will not let the wage of those who do good go to waste.'*

They said: 'By Allah, Allah has certainly preferred you above us and we have been in error.' (12: 90–1)

Yusuf did not blame them for what they had done. He said: *'May Allah forgive you. He is the Most Merciful of the Merciful.'* (12: 91)

Yusuf sends for Ya'qub

Yusuf longed to meet Ya'qub. How could he not

64

long to see him when they had been apart for such a long time? Why should he be patient now when the secret had been disclosed? How could he enjoy food and drink when his father was not enjoying food or drink or even sleep?

The secret was revealed, all was made known. Allah wanted to delight Ya'qub.

When Yusuf heard that Ya'qub had gone blind because of his great weeping and sorrow, he said: *'Take this shirt of mine and throw it over my father's face. He will recover his sight. Then bring me all of your family.'* (12: 93)

Ya'qub with Yusuf

As the messenger, ahead of the others, was carrying Yusuf's shirt back to Canaan, Ya'qub sensed Yusuf's scent on the air. He said: *'I smell the scent of Yusuf.'*

Those around him said: *'By Allah, you are in your old error.'* (12: 95)

But Ya'qub had spoken the truth. *When the bearer of good news came, he placed (the shirt) over Ya'qub's face and he saw once again. He said: 'Didn't I tell you that I know from Allah what you do not know?'* (12: 96) Now the brothers understood.

They said: 'Our father, ask forgiveness for us for our wrong actions. We have been in error.'

He said: 'I will ask my Lord to forgive you. He is All-Forgiving, All-Merciful.' (12: 97–8)

Then Ya'qub journeyed to Egypt and Yusuf received him. Their joy and happiness were great. It was a memorable and blessed day in Egypt.

Yusuf placed his parents on the throne. They all fell down prostrate before Yusuf, who said: *'This is the interpretation of my dream of long ago. My Lord has made it true. (12: 100) I saw eleven stars, the sun and the moon. I saw them bowing down to me.' (12: 4)*

Yusuf praised Allah greatly. He was very thankful for what had happened.

Ya'qub and his family stayed in Egypt for a long time. Ya'qub and his wife died in Egypt.

A good end

Although he was a ruler, with great power and authority, this did not distract Yusuf from Allah. It did not change him. He remembered Allah, worshipped Him and feared Him. He gave judgement according to the judgement of Allah. He carried out Allah's commands.

Yusuf did not want to die the death of a king. He did not want to be gathered with the kings. He wanted to die the death of a slave of Allah and to be gathered with the righteous.

This was Yusuf's prayer:

My Lord, You have given me a kingdom and taught me the interpretation of dreams. Creator of the heavens and the earth! You are my Guardian in this world and the next world. Make me die a Muslim and join me with the righteous. (12: 101)

Allah made him die a Muslim and joined him with his fathers, Ibrahim, Ishaq and Ya'qub, may Allah bless them and the Prophet Muhammad and grant them peace.

6. The Prophet Musa

From Canaan to Egypt

Ya'qub and his sons moved to Egypt because Yusuf the son of Ya'qub was the ruler of Egypt. Back in Canaan, they had herded their flocks, milked their sheep and sold their wool, while in Egypt even Yusuf's slaves and servants ate well and enjoyed themselves.

Yusuf sent for Ya'qub and his family, asking them to come from Canaan. He could not relish his food or drink when his father and brothers were not with him. How could he enjoy life when he alone was in Egypt? How could he live in a palace when his father and brothers lived in a tiny house in Canaan?

So Ya'qub and his sons came to Egypt. Yusuf welcomed them and was delighted to see them. The people of Egypt also welcomed the family of their lord, the family of their noble king. They loved this noble family because they loved Yusuf for his generosity and goodness to them, and because they saw he was a compassionate man who gave true counsel. They saw that Ya'qub too was a noble and generous father.

Ya'qub enjoyed great respect in Egypt. Its people were to him like his own sons. They were pleased that Ya'qub and his sons remained in Egypt, and Egypt became their homeland.

After Yusuf

After some time, Ya'qub died and was buried in Egypt. Yusuf grieved over him and so did the people of Egypt. It was as if they had lost their own father.

After a time, Yusuf also died. That was a terrible day for the people of Egypt. They were very sad and wept over him for a long time. They forgot their own sorrows in this greater sorrow. It was as if they had never been visited by any affliction before that day.

They buried Yusuf as well and consoled each other. They were all equal in their love for Yusuf. It was as if every child had lost a father and every adult had lost a brother. They went to Yusuf's sons and brothers to comfort them. They told them: 'Masters! Your loss today is no greater than our loss. We have lost a compassionate brother, a merciful and just master, in this man we buried today.

'He is the one who gave relief to the slaves and removed injustice from our country. He is the one who kept the great from harming the lowly and the strong from overpowering the weak. He is the one who helped those who had been wronged and gave refuge to those who were afraid, and fed those who were hungry.

'He is the one who guided us to the truth and called us to Allah. Before he came, we were like dumb animals who knew nothing about Allah or the Next World.

'He is the one who helped us during the famine. We were able to eat our fill while people in other countries were starving. We will never forget our noble king and we will never forget, lords, that you are his brothers and the people of his house.

'How happy our master was on the day when you came to Egypt! How happy we were to share our master's joy! The land is yours, and we will behave towards you just as we did when our master was alive.'

The Israelites in Egypt

And so it remained for a long time. The Egyptians remembered what they had said and acknowledged the virtue of the people of Canaan, also called the Israelites, people of nobility and wealth.

But later on things changed. The morals of the Israelites became corrupted and they stopped worshipping Allah and calling other people to worship Him. They slipped into the wicked ways of this world.

The Egyptian people also changed in their behaviour towards the Israelites. They began to look at them in a different way. The Israelites had become just like all other people. People began to envy the wealthy among them and to insult the poor.

The Egyptians believed that they were the people of the land and that Egypt belonged to them. Some of them considered Yusuf a foreigner who had come from Canaan when he was purchased by the Aziz of Egypt. They thought it was not right for a Canaanite to have ruled Egypt. Many of the people forgot the virtue, generosity and charity of Yusuf.

The pharaoh of Egypt

The Pharaohs came to the throne of Egypt, and they bore a deep hatred towards the Israelites. Then a particularly tyrannical man became the king. He did not know that the Israelites were the descendants of Prophets, nor that they were from the house of Yusuf, the noblest king of Egypt. He did not even consider them human beings entitled to mercy and justice.

He thought that his people, the Copts, were one race and the Israelites another. The Copts were a kingly race, created to rule; the Israelites were a race of slaves, created to serve.

Pharaoh treated the Israelites like work-animals who were there to serve and needed only to be fed and watered daily.

He was an arrogant tyrant who believed that no-one was higher than him. He did not believe in Allah. He used to say: *'I am your Lord Most High.'* (79: 24)

He was dazzled by his kingdom, his palaces, and his abundant provision. He used to say: *'Do I not possess the kingdom of Egypt and these rivers flowing beneath me? What, do you not see?'* (43: 51)

He behaved as if he was the successor to Nimrod, the King of Babylon. He became angry if he learned that anyone was thought of as being higher than him. He called on people to worship him and prostrate themselves before him, and they obeyed. But the Israelites refused because they believed in Allah and in His Messengers. Pharaoh therefore became very angry indeed with the Israelites.

Killing the children

A Coptic priest went to Pharaoh and told him: 'A child will be born among the Israelites at whose hands your kingdom will wither away.'

Pharaoh became mad with rage. He ordered his guards to kill every new-born boy of the Israelites. Pharaoh thought that he was the people's lord and master. He could kill whoever he pleased and let live whoever he pleased, like a sheep-owner who thinks he can kill or let live whichever of 'his' sheep he likes.

The guards searched throughout Egypt. Whenever they learned that a male child had been born among the Israelites, they took him and killed him.

Wolves living in the woods, and snakes and scorpions living in the desert, were ignored and safe. But no new-born boy of the Israelites was allowed to live in Pharaoh's kingdom.

Thousands of children were killed in front of their mothers and fathers. The day on which a male child was born to the Israelites was a day of sorrow and weeping. It was like a funeral day, a day for grief. Sometimes hundreds of children were killed on the same day.

Pharaoh had exalted himself in the land and had divided its inhabitants into sects, abasing a group of them, slaughtering their sons and letting their women live. He was one of those who work corruption. (28: 4)

The birth of Musa

But Allah wanted what Pharaoh feared and had been warned about, to take place. The child that Allah had destined to destroy Pharaoh's kingdom, and to bring people out of darkness into light, out of idol-worship into the worship of Allah, was born.

In spite of Pharaoh and his armies, Musa ibn 'Imran was born and survived.

In the Nile

Musa's mother was afraid for her beautiful son. How could she help it when the children's enemies were searching for him? How could she help being afraid when the guards had dragged dozens of children from their mothers' laps?

What could she do? Where could she hide her beautiful child when the guards had the sharp sight of crows and the keen smell of ants?

Then Allah helped Musa's mother and inspired her with the idea of putting him in a box and floating it down the Nile.

Glory be to Allah! How could a tender-hearted mother put her child into a box and then put it into the Nile? Who would suckle the child in the box? How would it breathe?

Musa's mother thought of all that, but she still put her trust in Allah and relied on Allah's protection. Her home was not able to protect the child any more than the box; there were guards everywhere, seeking out the new-born children.

So Musa's mother did what Allah had commanded her to do and put her beautiful child in a box and pushed it out into the water of the Nile. She was anxious, but then she became calm because of her trust in Allah.

So We inspired the mother of Musa: 'Suckle him. And, when you fear for him, put him into the river. Do not fear or sorrow. We will return him to you and make him one of the Messengers.' (28: 7)

In Pharaoh's palace

Pharaoh had many palaces on the banks of the Nile. He used to visit these palaces and would sometimes stroll along the banks of the river.

One day, Pharaoh and the Queen of Egypt were

72

walking along the river bank when they noticed a box being carried along by the current

'My lord, do you see that box?'

'How can there be a box in the Nile? It is a piece of wood which has fallen into the river?'

'No, my lord, it is a box.'

The box came nearer and the people said: 'Yes, it is a box!'

The King commanded one of his servants: 'Go and get this box!'

The servant brought the box to the King. They opened it and inside they found a beautiful, smiling boy.

Everyone was amazed. They wanted to hold him and look at him. Even Pharaoh was amazed and stared at him.

One of the servants said: 'It is an Israelite child. The King must kill it.'

When the Queen saw the child love filled her heart and she clasped him to her breast and kissed him. She pleaded with the King for him: *He will be a comfort to me and you! Do not kill him. Perhaps he will benefit us or we can take him for a son.'* (28: 9)

So Musa ibn 'Imran entered the palace of Pharaoh. He survived in spite of Pharaoh and his guards. The guards had not been guided to this Israelite child.

Allah wanted Pharaoh, 'the children's enemy,' to bring up the very child at whose hands his kingdom would be lost. Ah Pharaoh! How wrong he was about Musa! His minister, Haman, and his armies were wrong as well! *So the family of Pharaoh picked him out to be an enemy and a sorrow for them. Pharaoh, Haman and their armies were sinners.* (28: 8)

73

Who will suckle the child?

The child became the new plaything of the palace. Everyone came to look at him and kissed him. Everyone loved and praised him because the Queen loved and praised him.

How could the ladies of the palace not love him? How could the servants of the palace not love him? Everyone held him and kissed him because he was so beautiful.

The Queen looked for a wet-nurse to nurse the child. The nurse came and took the child, but he refused to take her milk and cried. The Queen got another nurse who came and took the child. Again, the child refused and cried. There was a third, fourth and fifth, but the child cried and refused their milk.

How puzzling! Why did the child refuse to feed?

The nurses tried hard to give the child their milk. They wanted to make the Queen happy and to win a reward from her. But Allah had made those nurses unlawful for him.

The child became the talk of the palace, the centre of everybody's attention:

'Sister, have you seen the new child?'

'Yes, I've seen him. A very beautiful child!'

'But an odd child! Not like other children. He will not take milk.'

'Whenever a nurse takes him, he cries and refuses to feed. Poor boy! How will he live? He will die!'

'Yes, it has been some days since he has fed.'

In his mother's arms

Musa's loving mother said to her daughter: 'Go and see if your brother is alive. Allah promised me that the child would be returned to me and that He would protect him.'

74

Musa's sister went to look for her brother. She heard the talk about a beautiful child in the King's palace. She went to the palace and listened to the women.

'Has the wet-nurse the Queen sent for come from Aswan?'

'Yes, my lady, but the child refused her and would not take her milk.'

'Goodness! What is wrong with this child? This is the sixth person the Queen has tried.'

'Yes, and they say that she is a very clean nurse and all children take milk from her.'

Musa's sister heard what was said. Then she said in a polite and friendly way: 'I know a woman in the town. The child will definitely accept milk from her.'

One woman said: 'I don't believe it. We have tried six wet-nurses, but the child has refused.'

Another woman said: 'Why don't we try a seventh? Why not?'

The news reached the Queen. She summoned the girl and said: 'Go and bring this woman.'

'Musa's mother came. A serving girl gave Musa to her. The child clung to her and began to accept milk from her as if he had been with her since birth. How could he not have, seeing as she was his own loving mother? How could he not want his own mother's milk when he had gone hungry for three days?

The Queen and the people of the palace were amazed.

Pharaoh was uneasy. He said: 'Why did the child accept this woman? Is she his real mother?'

Musa's mother said: 'My lord, I am a woman with a good smell, the smell of milk which every child accepts.'

Pharaoh was satisfied with her reply and paid her a wage.

Musa's mother then returned home with Musa in her arms: *So We returned him to his mother so that she might be comforted and not sorrow and so that she might know that the promise of Allah is true, but most people do not know.* (28: 13)

Return to Pharaoh's palace

After Musa was weaned, when he no longer needed his mother's milk, she returned him to the palace.

Musa grew up in the King's palace as a prince. That is how awe of kings and the wealthy was removed from his heart. He saw with his own eyes the luxury that Pharaoh and his family enjoyed and how the Israelites were oppressed for the sake of that luxury. He saw too how the Israelites went hungry so that Pharaoh's animals could eat. He saw how the Israelites were made to work like donkeys; how they were abused and humiliated with the worst possible treatment.

Musa saw these things every day and remained silent. But they angered Musa. How could he not feel anger at the abasement of his people and his family when they were the sons of Prophets and the sons of nobility? What wrong had the Israelites done, except that they were not Copts? Except that they were from Canaan? There was nothing wrong with that!

The fatal blow

Musa became a strong young man, and Allah gave him wisdom and knowledge.

Musa hated injustice. He favoured and sided with the weak and those who had been wronged. Every Prophet is like that.

One day Musa entered Pharaoh's city where people were busy either working or enjoying themselves. He found there two men fighting, one from the Israelites and the other from the Copts, the enemies of the Israelites.

The Israelite shouted to Musa to help him. Musa, trying to stop the two men fighting, hit the Copt. The Copt died.

Musa was filled with regret, knowing that it had all been Satan's doing. He turned to Allah in repentance. That is the way of all the Prophets. *He said: 'This is from Satan's doing. He is a clear, misguiding enemy.'* (28: 15)

Allah turned to Musa because he had not meant to kill the Copt. Musa praised Allah and said: 'Allah has blessed me and forgiven me. *I will never help wrongdoers.'* (28: 17)

The dead Copt was one of Pharaoh's servants, and the guards were searching for his slayer. Musa was fearful and watchful, not knowing when Pharaoh's guards would come for him. He feared being caught and taken before the tyrant.

The dead man became the talk of the town. Everyone was talking about it, but no-one knew who had slain him. Only Musa and the Israelite knew who had done it. Pharaoh was furious about the death of his servant and told his guards that they must find the man responsible.

The secret disclosed

The next day, Musa again saw the same Israelite in a fight with another Copt. The Israelite again cried out to Musa to help him.

Musa said: 'You are an impudent man. Here you are, still fighting and quarrelling with people. Shall I help you again? *You are clearly a quarrelsome person.'* (28: 18)

77

All the same, Musa wanted to stop the two men fighting and started towards them. However, the Israelite, seeing Musa's anger and hearing himself blamed, was afraid that Musa was about to strike him such as he had struck the Copt the previous day, and so he blurted out: *'Musa, do you want to kill me as you killed a man yesterday? You only mean to be a tyrant in the land. You do not want to be one of those who put things right.'* (28: 19)

Then the Copt ran away to tell the guards. When the news reached Pharaoh, he was angry. He said: 'Is this the boy who was our foster-child in the palace, the infant who was brought up by the Queen!'

Musa had not meant to kill the Copt. However Pharaoh and his guards would not take that into account, nor would they accept any excuse from Musa. Allah wanted to rescue Musa from Pharaoh's evil and his guards: Allah had decreed that Pharaoh would lose his kingdom, and the Israelites would be rescued, through Musa. Allah had decreed that Musa would bring people out of the worship of slaves (of Allah) into the worship of Allah the Exalted. How could that happen if the tyrant's guards were to lay their hands on him?

Pharaoh's ministers held a council and decided to have Musa put to death. A man, hearing of this went to Musa and told him the news: *'Depart! I am a sincere adviser to you.'* (28: 20)

Musa accepted this advice and hurried from the city. *He left there in fear and watchfulness, saying, 'My Lord, deliver me from the unjust people!'* (28: 21)

From Egypt to Midian

Where could Musa go when all of Egypt was Pharaoh's kingdom and Pharaoh's guards were everywhere?

78

Allah revealed to Musa to go to Midian, an Arab land, where Pharaoh's power did not reach. Midian was mostly desert and villages. It did not have the civilization, the castles and markets, of Egypt. But it was a happy land because it was far from Pharaoh and free of his tyrannical power.

How wonderful desert life is when it offers freedom and justice! How miserable civilization is when it offers slavery and abasement! No-one in Midian woke up in fear of the force and power of Pharaoh. No-one went to bed in Midian in fear of Pharaoh's guards or his evil.

Musa left Egypt in fear, watchful in case anyone pursued him. But the guards did not know he had left Egypt. He left in the name of Allah, calling on Allah for help. As he headed towards Midian, he said: *'It may be that my Lord will guide me on the right way.'* (28: 22)

In Midian

Musa reached Midian, not knowing anyone or being known by anyone. Where could he find shelter? Where could he spend the night? Musa was anxious, but he was certain that Allah would not let him die.

Musa came to a well where people got water for their animals. He found two girls there, holding back their sheep and waiting for the others to finish getting water so that they could have their turn.

Musa saw that and his heart was filled with the compassion and tenderness of a merciful father. He asked: 'Why aren't you getting water?'

They replied: 'We cannot take water for our sheep until the other people have got water because they are strong and we are weak, and because they are men and we are women.' Then, as if they knew that Musa was thinking, Why doesn't one of the men of your house get the water?, they added: *'Our father is an old man.'* (28: 23)

Compassion touched Musa and he drew water for them. Then they left.

Where would Musa go now? Where would he find shelter for the night? *Then he turned away to the shade and said: 'My Lord, I am certainly in need of whatever good You will send down on me.'* (28: 24)

The request

The two girls arrived home sooner than expected. Their father, a priest, was surprised and asked them: 'Why are you home so early, my daughters?'

The girls said: 'Allah sent a noble man to us who got us water.'

Their father realized that it must have been a stranger because no-one there had ever been kind to his daughters.

He said: 'Where did you leave this man?'

The girls replied: 'We left him at the well. He is a stranger and has no home here in Midian.'

The old man said: 'You did not do well, my daughters. A stranger has been good to you but he has no shelter in the land. Where will he find shelter for the night? We owe him the right of hospitality. One of you should go and bring him.'

Then one of the girls came to him, walking modestly. She said: 'My father invites you that he might repay you for the wage of your drawing water for us.' (28: 25)

Musa realized that Allah had answered his prayer and had turned towards him, so he should not refuse the offer. He walked ahead of the girl so that he would not be looking at her. This was a noble courtesy.

When they arrived, Musa was asked his name and from what country he had come.

The old man listened patiently. When Musa had finished, he said: *'Do not fear. You have escaped from unjust people.'* (28: 25)

Marriage

Musa stayed with the old man as an honoured guest, indeed like a beloved son. One of his daughters suggested to her father: *'Father, hire him. The best man you can hire is surely the one who is strong and trustworthy.'* (28: 26)

The old man asked: 'What do you know of his strength and trustworthiness, my daughter?'

She said: 'As for his strength, he lifted the lid from the well by himself and it normally takes several people to lift it. As for his trustworthiness, my father, he walked in front of me and did not look at me for the entire journey. Whoever you hire must be strong and trustworthy. If he is not strong, he will be too weak to work. If he is not trustworthy, his strength will not be of any use because he will be treacherous.'

The girl's words were what the old man wanted to hear, but he thought about the matter as a wise and caring father should. He thought to himself: Who could be a better son-in-law than this young man? Where will I find anyone better than this man? I have not found anyone else worthy of this in all Midian! Perhaps Allah has sent this youth to me to be my son-in-law and as a helper for me.

He addressed his thoughts to Musa in a kindly and courteous manner. He said: *'I would like you to marry one of my two daughters, provided you work for me for eight years. If you complete ten years, that will be on your own account. I do not desire to press you hard. You will find me one of the righteous, Allah willing.'* (28: 27)

Eight years to be spent with him was the bride-price the old man had asked. Perhaps he feared that Musa might take his daughter and leave straightaway. In this way he thought he could test Musa until he was sure of him and then he could bid him and his daughter farewell with peace of mind.

Musa agreed to these terms, trusting that it was from Allah and that Allah would bless him in it. Allah had led him to Midian and brought him to the old man and had put tenderness and love into his heart. But as Musa was wise and intelligent, he wanted to choose later on the number of years he stayed with the old man. *He said: 'That is between me and you. Whichever of the two terms I fulfil, it shall be no injustice on my part. Allah is the guardian of what we say.'* (28: 28)

To Egypt

When Musa had finished the term and departed with his household (28: 29), he and the priest said good-bye to one another. The priest said a prayer for him: 'Go with my blessing, my son. Go in Allah's protection, my daughter.'

Musa travelled with his family. The night was cold and dark. But where was fire to be found in the desert? What would they do if they could not find a fire to warm them or light to guide them? While they were travelling and Musa was searching, *he observed a fire. He said to his household, 'Stay here. I have observed a fire. Perhaps I will bring you a brand from it or I shall find guidance at the fire.'* (20: 10)

Musa went towards the fire, drawn to it by a powerful longing. *When he came to it, a voice cried: 'Musa, I am your Lord, so remove your shoes. You are in the Sacred Valley of Tuwa.'* (20: 12)

It was here that Allah spoke to Musa and revealed to him: *'I have chosen you, so listen to this revelation. I am Allah. There is no god but Me, so worship Me and perform the prayer for My remembrance. The Hour is coming.'* (20: 14–15)

Musa carried a staff which he used for various purposes. Allah the Exalted said: *'What is in your right hand, Musa?'* (20: 17)

Musa answered simply: *'This is my staff.'*

Then Musa began to list the uses of this staff because he wanted to speak to Allah for a long time. He said: *'I lean upon it and I use it to beat down the leaves to feed my sheep and I also have other uses in it.'* (20: 18)

He said: 'Throw it down, Musa!' (20: 19)

He threw it down and it became a slithering snake. (20: 20)

Allah said: 'Take it and do not fear. We will return it to its former state.' (20: 21)

Allah then gave Musa a second sign: *'Clasp your hand to your arm-pit. It will come out white without any evil. This is another sign.'* (20: 22)

'Go to Pharaoh, he has become insolent' (20: 24)

After that, Allah commanded Musa to begin the work for which he had been created. Pharaoh had become

83

insolent and was encouraging corruption in the land. Pharaoh's people had rejected Allah, and they too had a corruptive influence in the land. Allah does not like His slaves to refuse to believe in Him. He does not like corruption in the land. He wanted Musa to go to Pharaoh and Pharaoh's subjects: *They were an ungodly people.* (28: 32)

But how could Musa go back there and confront the tyrant? He had killed a Copt, and had been forced to leave Egypt in fear of his life. Moreover, he was well-known to the guards and the people of the palace.

He said: *'My Lord, I killed one of them and I fear that they will kill me.'* (28: 33)

Allah knew all of this but wanted Musa to go in spite of it: *'Go to the people of the evildoers, the people of the Pharaoh. Will they not be godfearing?'*

He said: 'My Lord, I fear that they will deny me and my breast will be constricted and my tongue will not be loosened, so send for Harun (to help me). They also hold against me a wrong action, and I fear that they will kill me.'

He said: 'No, indeed. Go, both of you, with Our signs. We will be with you, listening. Go to Pharaoh and say, "I am the Messenger of the Lord of all the worlds. Send the Children of Israel with us."' (26: 10–17)

Allah advised Musa and Harun to be gentle and kind with Pharaoh. Allah likes to be kind to His enemies for a time, so that they may reform themselves: *'Speak gently to him. He may heed or fear.'* (20: 44)

Before Pharaoh

Musa and Harun went to Pharaoh and stood in his Council, calling him to Allah. The tyrant became angry at

Musa's boldness and said with disdain and arrogance: 'Who are you, young man, to stand up in my Council and admonish me? Aren't you the boy whom we pulled out of the water? *Did we not bring you up among us as a child? Did you not stay with us for many years of your life? Then you did the deed you did, being one of the ungrateful!'* (26: 18–19)

Musa did not get angry or deny this. He did not argue or make excuses. He spoke plainly and with great dignity. *He said: 'Indeed I did it then, for I was one of those who are astray. So I fled from you, fearing you. But my Lord gave me judgement and made me one of the Messengers.'* (26: 20–1)

Musa went on: 'Pharaoh, you were gracious to me in that you brought me up. But you do not see why I came into your hands or why you were able to bring me up. If you had not given the command for the children to be killed, my mother would not have put me into the Nile and I would not have come into your hands. Is that then a blessing to be remembered and weighed against your injustice and cruelty? You treated all my people as if they were donkeys and beasts. You treated them like dogs. You inflicted terrible punishment on them.

'Certainly you brought me up, but *that is a blessing which you reproach me with, having enslaved the Children of Israel.* (26: 22) Then what virtue can you claim for yourself for looking after one of their children? That also only came about through ignorance and error!'

Calling to Allah

Pharaoh was speechless. He tried to bluster his way out of it by asking: *'What is the Lord of all the worlds* that I hear you mentioning?'

He said: *'The Lord of the heavens and the earth and what is between them if you have certainty.'* (26: 23–4)

Pharaoh was angered by Musa's reply and wanted to provoke the people of the Council against him. So *he said to those about him: 'Do you not hear?'* (26: 25)

Musa continued: *'Your Lord and the Lord of your fathers, the ancients.'* (26: 26)

Pharaoh could not contain his anger. *He said: 'Your messenger who has been sent to you is possessed!'* (26: 27)

Musa still did not stop speaking. He said: *'The Lord of the East and the West and what is between them if you have understanding.'* (26: 28)

Pharaoh wanted to distract Musa from this argument that was so hard for him, and to provoke his Council to anger. *He asked Musa: 'What about the former generations?'* (20: 51) His thinking was: If Musa says that the forefathers knew the truth, then I will say, 'They worshipped idols.' If Musa says that they were misguided and foolish, the people of the Council will become angry and say, 'Musa has cursed our forefathers!'

But Musa was more intelligent than Pharaoh. He possessed a light from his Lord. He said: *'The knowledge of them is with my Lord in a Book. My Lord does not err nor does He forget.'* (20: 52)

Then Musa went on to say what Pharaoh had been trying to avoid hearing himself, and prevent others from hearing. He said: *'My Lord does not err nor does He forget, the One who appointed the earth to be a couch for you and threaded roads in it for you and sent down water from heaven.'* (20: 52–3)

Pharaoh was confused. He did not know what to say. Then he tried to frighten Musa. *He said: 'If you take a god other than me, I will make you one of the imprisoned!'* (26: 29)

Musa's miracles

When Pharaoh had shot that bolt, Musa wanted to hit him with Allah's bolt. *He said, 'What, even if I bring you something clear?'* (26: 30)

Pharaoh said: 'Bring it then if you are one of the truthful.' (26: 31)

So Musa threw down his staff and it was a manifest snake. He drew forth his hand and it was white to the viewers. (26: 32–3)

Pharaoh found something to say only to his companions. *He said to the Council around him: 'This man is a cunning sorcerer.'* (26: 34)

The people of the Council agreed. *They said: 'This is a manifest sorcerer.'*

Musa said: 'What, do you say this to the truth, when it has come to you, "Is this sorcery?" Sorcerers do not prosper.' (10: 77)

Then Pharaoh's people shot another bolt at Musa. *They said: 'Have you come to us to turn us from what we found our fathers doing? Does domination in the land belong to you two? We do not believe you.'* (10: 78)

Then, Pharaoh tried to alarm the Council about Musa. He said: *'He wants to drive you out of your land by sorcery. What do you command?'* (26: 25)

The Council then suggested to the King that he should assemble the best sorcerers in his kingdom and that they should use their magic against Musa. The King agreed. A proclamation was made throughout the kingdom: 'Whoever knows magic should come to the King.'

Sorcerers gathered from every corner of the kingdom. Feast Day was set as the date for the contest. *The people were asked: 'Will you gather?'*

Perhaps we will follow the sorcerers if they are the winners.' (26: 40)

To the square

The people left their houses in the morning and walked to the square in throngs. Children, young and old people, men and women, all were going to the square. Only the sick and the very old were left at home.

All the talk was of sorcery and the names of sorcerers.

'Has the Great Wizard of Aswan* come as well?'

'Yes, and the Wizard of Luxor* and the famous sorcerer of Giza*.'

'Brother, who do you think will win?'

'Egypt is putting forward her very best! Do you think anyone can beat them?'

'How can Musa and his brother beat them? Where did they learn magic?'

'He grew up in the King's palace and he left Egypt in fear for his life and then he spent some years in Midian.'

'So where did he learn magic?'

'In Egypt? Never!'

'In Midian? We have not heard that they possess that science there.'

The Israelites came, torn between hope and despair, perhaps more in a state of despair, saying, 'May Allah show mercy to 'Imran's son! May Allah help the Israelites!'

The sorcerers came forward in all their pride and arrogance, clothed in colourful garments, carrying their staffs and ropes. They were laughing and joking for this

---

*Names of towns in ancient Egypt.

was the day of their science: today the King would see their art! Today the people would see their excellence!

When the sorcerers came, they said to Pharaoh: 'Shall we have a wage if we are the victors?'

He said: 'Yes, and you shall be among those near-stationed.' (26: 41–2)

Such are the rewards and gifts offered by kings! That is how good men are deceived and trapped. But the sorcerers were happy with Pharaoh's promises.

Between truth and falsehood

When the sorcerers were ready, *Musa told them: 'Throw down what you will throw.'*

They threw their ropes and staffs and said: 'By the might of Pharaoh we will win.' (43: 44)

Then the people saw a marvellous sight: there were snakes slithering in the square. Startled, they drew back with shouts of 'Snakes! Snakes!' Some women and children screamed in alarm. The cry of 'Snakes! Snakes!' filled the square.

Musa saw the same thing that the people saw and was amazed. *It seemed to him through their sorcery that their ropes and staffs were sliding.* (20: 66)

Fear crept into Musa's heart. This was the day of the contest. In a contest a man is either honoured or dishonoured! If the sorcerers were to win, may Allah not decree that! If Musa were to be defeated, may Allah not allow that! What would he do then? We seek refuge with Allah!

The defeat of Musa would not only mean the defeat of one man, but the defeat of a Religion at the hands of a king, the defeat of the truth by falsehood.

Allah would never decree that! Allah would never permit that! Allah gave Musa courage and said: *'Do not be afraid. You certainly have the upper hand. Throw down what is in your right hand. It will swallow up what they have fashioned. They have only fashioned the guile of a sorcerer. The sorcerer does not prosper wherever he goes.'* (20: 68–9)

Musa said: *'What you have brought is sorcery. Allah will bring it to nothing. Allah does not uphold the deeds of those who do corruption. Allah verifies the truth by His words, even though the wrong-doers are averse.'* (10: 81–2)

Musa threw down his staff and it swallowed up their lying invention. (26: 45) *The truth came to pass and what they were doing was proved false.* (7: 118)

The sorcerers could hardly believe what they saw: 'What is this? We know sorcery and what it is based on. We know magic in all its forms. We are the masters, the leaders, of the art! But this does not come from sorcery!

'If it had been sorcery, we would have beaten it with sorcery, confronting science with science. But our sorcery fades away in the face of this. It melts away as dew melts before the sun. Where is this from? This must be from Allah!'

The sorcerers were satisfied that Musa was a Prophet and that Allah had given him a miracle. They cried out aloud: *'We believe in the Lord of Harun and Musa.' The sorcerers fell down in prostration. They said: 'We believe in the Lord of all the worlds, the Lord of Musa and Harun.'* (26: 48)

Pharaoh's threat

Pharaoh became wild with rage. He leapt to his feet and sat down again, helpless with anger. The very thing he feared had happened! He had brought the best sorcerers to defeat Musa but the sorcerers had become Musa's followers! Also the people were now the first to believe in Musa! His arrows were turned back against him.

Pharaoh had believed that he controlled minds just as he controlled bodies, that he had power over hearts just as he had power over tongues. No-one in Egypt was allowed to believe or accept anything without his permission. He spoke with pride and arrogance: *'You have believed in Him before I gave you leave?'* (26: 49)

Pharaoh then shot another arrow, saying, *'He is your chief, the same one who taught you sorcery!'* (26: 49)

Then he struck at them again, accusing them of a plot: *'This is a trick you have devised in the city in order to expel its people from it. Now you shall know!'* (7: 123)

Then he struck at them with a third poisoned arrow, the final arrow in the quiver of an earthly ruler. He said: *'I shall cut off your hands and feet alternately and I will crucify all of you.'* (26: 50–1)

These believers met all the arrows with the shield of belief and patience. They said: *'No matter! Indeed we are turning to our Lord. We ardently hope for our Lord to forgive us our sins and we are the first of the believers.'* (26: 50–1)

They spoke with firm belief: *'We believe in our Lord that He might forgive us our sins and the sorcery you forced us to practise. Allah is better and endures forever. Whoever comes to his Lord as a sinner will have Jahannam* (Hell). *There he will neither die nor live. Whoever comes to Him*

91

as a believer, having performed righteous actions, those will have the highest degrees, the gardens of Eden with rivers flowing underneath them. That is the reward of those who purify themselves.' (20: 74–6)

Pharaoh's folly

Pharaoh was deeply worried by Musa. He spent sleepless nights, unable even to enjoy his food or drink. Other people also provoked him and he became even angrier. *They said: 'Will you leave Musa and his people to work corruption in the land and leave your gods?'*

He said: 'We shall slaughter their sons and let their women live. We are in power over them!' (7: 127)

Anxious to stop the Israelites and the Egyptians believing in Musa, *Pharaoh proclaimed among his people: 'O people! Do I not possess the kingdom of Egypt and these rivers flowing under me? What, do you not see? Am I better or this man, who is contemptible and scarcely makes things clear?'* (43: 51–2)

Pharaoh then said, with a great show of composure: *'O Council! I do not know that you have any other god than me!'* (28: 38)

It was as if he had reflected deeply on the matter and was offering good advice to his people. He said: *'Haman, kindle me a fire upon the clay and build me a tower that I may climb up to Musa's God, for I think that he is one of the liars.'* (28: 38)

Haman kindled a fire on the clay. He built a tower, but up to where? Haman grew weary and the workers grew weary. Pharaoh could not build high enough to reach the clouds, let alone the moon, not the moon let alone the sun, not the sun let alone the stars, not the stars let alone the sky.

Pharaoh was disappointed and ashamed. He was powerless to do his will. He did not know that *Allah created the earth and the highest heavens. To Him belongs whatever is in the heavens and whatever is in the earth and whatever is between them and what is under the earth.* (20: 4–6)

He is the One who is God in the heavens and God in the earth. (43: 84)

Pharaoh decided that the only way to beat Musa was to kill him. *Pharaoh said: 'Let me kill Musa and let him call to his Lord. I fear that he may change your religion or he may cause corruption to appear in the land.'* (40: 26)

A believer from Pharaoh's people

While Pharaoh was plotting how to kill Musa, a certain man, a believer from among Pharaoh's people, who had kept his belief hidden, said: *'Are you going to kill a man just because he says, "My Lord is Allah", when he has brought you the clear proofs from your Lord?'* (40: 28)

This man then said: 'Why do you oppose Musa and seek to harm him? If you do not believe him, then leave him alone and let him go his way: *If he is a liar, then his lie is on his own head . . .* (40: 28) If you harm him and attack him and he turns out truly to be a Prophet, then woe will befall you. *If he is telling the truth, some of what he warns (you of) will befall you.'* (40: 28)

'My brothers, do not be dazzled by your kingdom. Do not be dazzled by your strength and armies!'

'O my people, you have the kingdom today, being masters in the land. But who will help us against Allah's punishment if it comes upon us?' (40: 29)

Pharaoh's answer was: *'I only let you see what I myself see and I only guide you on the path of guidance.'* (40: 29)

The believer wanted to warn his people about a terrible punishment and the fate of those who are unjust. He said: *'O my people, I fear for you the like of the day of the Parties, the like of what happened to the people of Nuh, 'Ad and Thamud and those after them. Allah does not desire injustice for His servants.'* (40: 31)

This sensible man tried to make them fear the Day of Judgement. And how awesome is that Day!

A day when a man shall flee from his brother, his mother and his father, and his wife and his sons. Every man on that day will have concern enough for himself to make him heedless (of others). (80: 34–7)

Friends on that day will be enemies to one another, except for the God-fearing. (43: 67)

There will be no kinship between them and they will not question one another. (23: 101)

On the day when the All-Powerful King calls out: *'Whose is the Kingdom today?' 'Allah's, the One, the All-Mighty.'* (40: 16)

The day when people are alarmed and shout and call to one another, the day when they turn around in retreat, they will have no protector against Allah.

The sensible man then said: *'O my people, I fear for you the Day of Invocation, the day when you turn about in retreat, having no protector against Allah. Whoever Allah misguides has no guide for him.'* (40: 33)

He continued: 'Allah gave you a blessing, but you did not recognize its excellence, nor did you value it as it should have been valued, until it had gone. Then you regretted it. That was the Prophet Yusuf, may Allah's peace

94

and blessing be upon him, whom you did not recognize and whose worth you did not esteem.

'But when he died, you said, "Glory be to Allah! There will never be a Prophet like Yusuf! There will never be a king like Yusuf! There will never be a man like Yusuf! Who will we have for a Prophet after him? Who will we ever have like him? No-one! There will never be anyone like him!"

'Yusuf brought you the clear signs before, but you continued in doubt concerning what he had brought you until you said, "Allah will never send a messenger after him." (40: 34)

'That is how you will behave after this Prophet as well, and again you will regret it!'

The man's good advice

The man warned his people and gave them of his love and best counsel.

The man who believed said: 'O my people, follow me. I will guide you in the path of guidance.' (40: 38)

He knew that the people were intoxicated with the life of this world and that Pharaoh was dazzled by his kingdom and power. But the life of this world is nothing but a dream, a fading shadow.

This man knew what kept people from following Musa. It was because they were drunk with the pleasures of this life. The drunkard, when he is drunk, is not afraid, and he is not aware. That is why these people could not hear Musa's voice. But the man still wanted to call their attention to this heedlessness. He said: *'O my people, the life of this world is only a brief enjoyment. The Next World is the Lasting Abode.'* (40: 39)

Those of his people who were ignorant began to call him back to unbelief and idol-worship, back to the religion of their ancestors. When he said to them, 'Come to Allah,' they said, 'Return to the religion of your ances-tors.'

They insisted so much that he said to them: *'O my people, how is it that I call you to salvation while you call me to the Fire? You call me to reject Allah and associate with Him that of which I have no knowledge, while I call you to the Mighty, the Forgiving.'* (40: 41–2) He asked them: 'What Prophet has come from your gods? What book has been sent down? Who has called you to what you believe? *These are names you have named, you and your fathers. Allah has not sent down any authority for them.* (53: 23)

'It is the Messengers of Allah who call to Allah. Among them were Ibrahim, peace be upon him, and Yusuf. And Musa is the Prophet of Allah.

'There is a sign of Allah in every thing, a call to Him in every place. While there can be *'no doubt that what you call me to does not have any claim, either in this world or in the Next World.'* (40: 43)

When the man despaired of guiding them and was exasperated with their stupidity, he left them, saying, *'You will remember what I told you. I entrust my affair to Allah. Allah sees His slaves.'* (40: 44)

The people of Pharaoh became angry and wanted to kill him, but Allah protected him and destroyed his enemies.

Allah guarded him against the evils they devised and an evil punishment encompassed the people of Pharaoh. (40: 45)

Pharaoh's wife

Pharaoh believed that he was the master of people's minds in the same way that he was of their bodies, that he had power over people's hearts as he had power over their tongues. No-one in Egypt was allowed to believe anything or accept anything without his permission.

When anyone believed in Musa, even in the furthest part of his kingdom, Pharaoh became furious. He leapt to his feet and sat down again, he thundered and raged. He would say: 'How can he believe in Musa before I have given him permission! He lives in comfort in my kingdom and now he rebels against me! He consumes my provision and now he is ungrateful to me! I have a better right to every single man in Egypt than the man himself has!'

Pharaoh forgot that he was living in comfort in Allah's kingdom and yet he was rebelling against Him. He was consuming Allah's provision and yet was ungrateful to Him.

Allah showed him a sign in his own house, within his own family. Allah showed him that He alone is the King of people's minds in the same way that He is the King of their bodies, that He alone has power over people's hearts as He has power over their tongues. Allah can come between a man and his family, between a man and his heart.

Belief entered Pharaoh's house without him being aware of it, showing that he was not in control of anything. Pharaoh's wife believed in Allah and rejected Pharaoh. She believed in Musa in spite of her husband, the King of Egypt. She knew Pharaoh better than anyone else, and Pharaoh loved her better than anyone else, but she believed in Musa and in the message he brought from Allah.

Pharaoh's guards could not do anything; they were unaware of this event. Indeed, Pharaoh, who was closest to the Queen, was himself unaware of it. Even if Pharaoh had known, what could he have done? He owned people's bodies, but not their minds. He had power over people's tongues, but no power over their hearts.

A woman should obey her husband, but no-one should obey a creature who is in rebellion against his Creator. Children should obey their parents and be dutiful to them, but they do not have to obey them in the associating of things with Allah: *If they try to make you associate with Me what you have no knowledge of, do not obey them. Keep their company in this world kindly and follow the path of the one who turns to Me. Then you will return to Me and I will tell you what you were doing.* (31: 15)

Pharaoh's wife was correct in her belief. She worshipped Allah in the house of Allah's enemy. She declared to Allah that she was innocent of what Pharaoh was doing. Allah was pleased with Pharaoh's wife and saved her from Pharaoh and his actions. Allah made her an example for the believers through her faith and courage.

Allah made an example of Pharaoh's wife for those who believe when she said, 'My Lord, build me a house with You in the Garden and save me from Pharaoh and his deeds and save me from the unjust people.' (66: 11)

The testing of the Israelites

As people knew that Pharaoh was hostile to the Israelites, they sided with him and displayed their hostility towards them also. Their children were rude to the Israelites and their dogs chased them. Every day brought a new trial. Every night brought a new disaster.

Musa consoled his people and advised them to be patient. He told them: *'Pray for Allah's help and be patient. The land belongs to Allah. He will bequeath it to whomever of His slaves He wills. The final outcome belongs to those who fear Allah.'* (7: 128)

The Israelites disliked this trial and persecution and told Musa: 'You haven't helped us at all! You haven't spared us anything! *We were harmed before you came to us and after you came to us.'* (7: 129)

But Musa was not alarmed. He did not despair. *He said, 'Perhaps your Lord will destroy your enemy and will appoint you successors in the land, so that He can see how you act.'*

Musa said: 'O my people, if you believe in Allah, you must trust in Him, if you have surrendered yourselves to Him.'

They said: 'We have put our trust in Allah, our Lord. Do not make us a temptation for the wrong-doing people. Save us by Your mercy from the people of the unbelievers.' (10: 84–6)

Pharaoh had forbidden the Israelites from worshipping Allah. He was angry when he saw them worshipping Him or praying to Him. He had forbidden them from making mosques for Allah in his land. It enraged him to see Allah being worshipped in his land.

How ignorant of Allah he was! The land belongs to Allah, not to any Pharaoh. Who could be more unjust than someone who forbids Allah's slaves from worshipping Allah in Allah's land. Who could be more unjust than someone who calls on people to worship himself in Allah's land?

But Pharaoh could not keep people from doing whatever they liked in their own homes! Allah commanded

99

the Israelites on the tongue of Musa: *'Make your houses a direction for men to pray, and perform the prayer.'* (10: 87)

Pharaoh and his guards were powerless to prevent the Israelites worshipping Allah. Who can come between a slave and his Lord? Who can come between a Muslim and the worship of Allah?

Famines

As Pharaoh became more tyrannical and heedless, Allah wanted to warn him. Allah does not like His slaves to disbelieve. He does not like corruption in the land.

Pharaoh was very silly. Wise words and warnings were wasted on him. Certain donkeys do not take any notice until they are beaten. Allah wanted to make Pharaoh take notice.

Egypt was a green, fertile land, a land of blessings and fruits, a land where grain grew in abundance. You remember how Egypt helped distant lands in the years of famine during the time of Yusuf and how Egypt helped the people of Syria and Canaan. The Nile gives water to Egypt and irrigates its crops. It is a source of joy and blessing to the people of that land.

Pharaoh and the Egyptian people thought that the Nile was the key to their provision and the Nile made Egypt so rich that it did not need rain or anything else. They did not know that the keys of provision are with Allah and that Allah gives provision to whoever He wills, and withholds it from whoever He wills. They did not know that the Nile flows and floods at Allah's command.

Allah commanded the Nile, and its waters receded and disappeared into the ground. Without those waters how could the crops of the Egyptian people be irrigated? The fruits of the land disappeared and its grain dwindled. There was famine after famine.

Pharaoh was seen to be powerless. Haman was seen to be powerless. Pharaoh's guards were seen to be unable to devise any plot. Then the people of Egypt knew that Pharaoh was not their Lord and that provision was in the hands of Allah. But that did not benefit Pharaoh or his people, it did not wake them up. Satan was able to come between them and the warning lesson they had been given. They decided: 'These famines and bad years are bad luck which come from Musa and his people.'

How strange an excuse! Had Musa not been there before? Had not the Israelites been there for a long time? It was bad luck brought about by their own actions, their own unbelief. But Pharaoh and his people were stubborn and said: 'We will not submit to this magic. *Whatever sign you bring to us to bewitch us, we will not believe you.'* (7: 132)

Five signs

Allah then sent them another sign. He sent rains and the Nile overflowed. It rained and rained until the fields were so flooded that the crops were washed away. The rain became a curse. The people complained about the lack of it and now they were complaining about too much.

Then Allah sent locusts which devoured the crops and fields and stripped the trees. They left nothing behind. The armies of Pharaoh could not fight the army of Allah. How could they fight them when neither swords nor spears were of any use against them?

The people of Egypt saw that Pharaoh was weak and that Haman was powerless and that the plots of the guards were of no use. But they did not reflect! They did not take note!

Allah then sent another army, an army of lice. He gave the lice power over them. We seek refuge with Allah! Lice in their beds, in their clothes, on their heads, in their hair! They spent sleepless nights looking for lice and cursing them until morning. How could they fight them, when neither swords nor spears affected them. Their armies and guards could not save them.

Then Allah sent frogs. There were frogs in their storage vessels for food and drink. They found frogs even in their clothes. The frogs made their lives a misery. The frogs multiplied and were found all over their houses. They croaked all night. One jumped here and another hopped there. Whenever they killed one, ten more appeared. The guards were powerless against the frogs.

Allah then sent a fifth sign against them: blood. Their noses bled and this enfeebled and exhausted them. Their doctors were unable to treat them. No medicine helped.

Whenever they saw a sign, they said to Musa: 'Ask your Lord to remove this affliction from us. We repent and believe, and we will send the Israelites away with you.' But when Allah removed the affliction from them, they broke their promise.

So we let loose on them the flood and the locusts and lice, the frogs and the blood, distinct signs. But they became proud and were a sinful people. (7: 133)

The departure

The Israelites realized that they could not live any longer in Egypt. Though it was a vast land, what use could they make of its fertility and blessings while they were in prison suffering all sorts of torment and humiliation? How long could they be patient? Were they not human beings suffering injury and pain?

Allah revealed to Musa that he should lead the Israelites out of Egypt. Pharaoh's guards heard of this and informed Pharaoh.

One night Musa led the twelve tribes of Israelites, each with its own leader, out of Egypt towards the Holy Land. The road to Syria was direct and well-known. It went between the two lands. Musa had already travelled it when he went to Midian, and again when he returned to Egypt.

But Musa meant to go one way while Allah intended him to go another. What Allah wanted was what happened. In the darkness Musa took the wrong road and, when Musa made this mistake, what Allah willed to happen happened. Musa intended to take the Israelites to the north. However, they found themselves heading towards the east. They found themselves on the shores of the Red Sea.

'O Protector! O Veiler! Where are we?'

The answer was: 'We are on the seashore.'

As the dawn broke, they looked back and saw a huge cloud of dust. Coming after them was a great army which filled the horizon. Voices were raised, saying, 'Son of 'Imran! What did you have against us to make you plot to kill us? You have brought us to the edge of the sea so that Pharaoh can kill us here like rats, when there is no way of escape.

'We know of no wrong that we have done to you, so why are you taking revenge like this? Wasn't the hardship and affliction we have already endured enough for you without you bringing us here? We have the sea in front of us and the enemy behind us. There is no outcome for us but death.'

Then the Israelites were seized by despair and their voices were stilled. Everyone was afraid. Even firm mountains would have had the right to tremble.

But Musa's faith in his Lord was not shaken. The people heard a voice filled with the majesty of prophethood: 'No, but my Lord is with me. He will guide me.' (26: 62)

Then Allah commanded Musa to strike the sea with his staff. He struck it and the sea divided. The waters rose up like mountains one on either side. There were twelve paths, one for each tribe. The people crossed unharmed and reached the land of safety and peace.

Pharaoh's drowning

Pharaoh saw how the Israelites had crossed the sea in safety. He said to his armies, 'Look how the sea divides freely at my command so that I can catch these fugitives.'

Pharaoh advanced with his armies and the Israelites were in fear once again. 'Here is the enemy, the tyrant, intending to cross over to us! Nothing will keep him from us! He will catch us and take us back to Egypt in captivity or slaughter us as exiles in the desert!'

Musa thought to strike the land with his staff so that it would once more become sea as it had been before. But Allah revealed to him: 'Leave the sea alone. *They are a drowned army.*' (44: 24)

When Pharaoh and his armies reached the middle of the path through the sea, the sea flooded back over them. Only now, with the waves crashing around him, did Pharaoh face up to the truth. *Until, when drowning overtook him, he said, 'I believe that there is no god except the One in whom the Israelites believe, and I am one of the believers.'* (10: 90)

104

How deep he was in error! *Allah will not turn towards those who do wrong actions until, when one of them is near death, he says, 'I repent now.'* (4: 18) *The day that certain of the signs of your Lord do come, no good will it do to a soul to believe in them then, if it believed not before, nor earned righteousness through its faith.* (6: 158)

Pharaoh was told: *'Now? When you rebelled before and were one of the corrupters!'* (10: 91)

Pharaoh drowned in the sea.

The tyrant who had ordered the deaths of thousands of children was dead. The tyrant who had had thousands of people killed, cruelly and without mercy, was dead. The King of Egypt died far away from his throne, far away from his power, without anyone to console him or anyone to weep for him.

Some of the Israelites, aware of Pharaoh's great power began to doubt if he had really died: 'Perhaps Pharaoh is not dead. Did we not use to see him go for days without eating or drinking.' Then the sea cast up Pharaoh's body on the shore and they were sure that he was dead.

Allah the Exalted said to Pharaoh: *'Today We will deliver you with your body so that you will be a sign for those after you.'* (10: 92) The body of Pharaoh was a sign for those who are able to see, a lesson for those who are capable of learning a lesson.

Pharaoh's army drowned to the last man. They had left Egypt behind them and did not find a cubit for burial in all its vast land.

How many gardens and fountains they left behind, sown fields, and how noble a station, and what blessings they delighted in! Just like that, and We bequeathed them

105

to another people. Neither the heaven nor the earth wept for them and they were not given a reprieve. (44: 25–9)

In the desert

The Israelites reached the land of security and peace and breathed its air as noble and free men. There were neither Pharaoh nor Haman nor their guards to fear. They walked in safety, fearing none but Allah.

But they were city people and the sun in the desert was too hot for them. They did not have tents which could shelter them from the sun. Yet they were the guests of Allah, and His generosity is greater than any other's generosity. Allah commanded the clouds to give them shade. The clouds went with them wherever they went and stopped whenever they stopped.

The Israelites were thirsty and there was no water in the desert, no river or well. They went to Musa and complained to him as a child complains to its mother and asks for her help. They complained of their thirst.

Musa called on his Lord. To whom else could he turn? Allah said: *'Strike the rock with your staff.' Twelve springs gushed forth from it. All the people knew their drinking-place.* (2: 60)

The Israelites were hungry and complained to Musa as a child complains to its mother and asks for her help. They said: 'You brought us out of Egypt, the land of fruits and produce, the land of blessings and good things. Who will give us food in this desert?'

Musa called on his Lord. Who else did he have besides Him? Allah sent down food on them. He sent down sweet things for them onto the leaves of the trees and He sent birds to them which could easily be taken

106

from the trees. These things were *manna* and *salwa,* Allah's hospitality to the Israelites in the desert.

The ingratitude of the Israelites

But the tastes and morals of the Israelites had become corrupted by their long enslavement. They could not make up their minds about anything, and were constantly discontented. They were like spoilt children. They showed little gratitude and had many complaints. They were quick to become bored, wanting what they were forbidden and hating what they were given. It was not long before they told Musa: 'We don't like only having one kind of food. We do not like this meat and this sweet stuff. We want vegetables and green herbs. *Musa, we will not endure one sort of food. Ask your Lord to bring forth for us of what the earth produces of its green herbs, cucumbers, corn, lentils and onions.* (2: 61)

Musa was amazed at this strange request and said in a voice filled with disapproval: *'Would you take what is inferior in exchange for what is better?'* (2: 61)

Are herbs and vegetables better than birds and sweets that no human hand has touched? Is the food of peasants better than the food of kings?

But the Israelites continued to ask for vegetables and green herbs. Then Musa said: 'What you ask for exists in every village and city. *Get down to a township. There you will have what you ask for.'* (2: 61)

The stubbornness of the Israelites

The Israelites were like spoilt, stubborn children who, when they are told to do something, make fun of it and do the opposite. It is as if they think it is clever to change whatever they are told. So when they are told, 'Stand up,' they sit down; when they are told, 'Sit down,' they stand up. When they are told, 'Be quiet,' they speak; when they are told, 'Speak,' they are silent.

They had wanted to be settled in a village and eat tasty food made of vegetables and green herbs. But when they were told: *'Enter this township and eat freely from it wherever you like and enter the gate in prostration and say, "Repentance." We will forgive you your errors and increase the good-doers.'* (2: 58), they were angry at this command from Allah. They entered the village reluctantly.

'Those who did wrong substituted words other than those which had been said to them.' (2: 59) So Allah sent down affliction on them and spread a plague among them so that they died like rats.

When they were given a command, they asked many questions and disputed it, so avoiding doing what they were asked to do.

A murder took place among the Israelites and they were worried about it. They could not find the killer. They went to Musa and said: 'Prophet of Allah, help us in this case and ask Allah to make it clear to us who the killer is.'

The cow

Musa called on his Lord who revealed to him that he should command them to make a sacrifice of a cow. For the Israelites, this was as if some misfortune had befallen them, so they began to question and mock.

When Musa said to his people: 'Allah commands you to sacrifice a cow,' they said, 'Are you mocking us?' He said, 'I seek refuge in Allah lest I be one of the ignorant.' (2: 67)

Now they asked Musa many questions. *They said: 'Ask your Lord for us to make clear to us what she may be.'*

He said: *'He says that she is a cow neither old nor virgin, but between the two. Do as you are commanded.'* (2: 68)

But they did not stop with that question. They began to ask about the cow's colour. *They said: 'Ask your Lord for us to make clear to us what her colour is.'*

He said: *'He says that she is a golden cow, bright in colour, delighting those who see.'* (2: 69)

Then, when they could not think of a definite question, they came up with a vague, general question. *They said: 'Ask your Lord for us to make clear to us what she may be. All cows are much the same to us. If Allah wills, we will be guided.'*

He said: *'He says that she is a cow not trained to plough the earth nor irrigate the crops, sound, no flaw in her.'* (2: 70)

They accepted this time because they said, *'If Allah wills, we will be guided,'* so they were guided.

But their questions had made things difficult for them. If they had sacrificed any cow, that would have been enough. But they looked for difficulties for themselves, so Allah provided for them.

They searched for a medium-sized golden cow, radiant in colour, which had not tilled the earth nor irrigated a field, sound, without flaw. This sort of cow was very rare. The cows were either old or virgin. Or they were medium-sized, but not golden. Or they were medium-sized and golden, but their colour was not radiant. Or they were medium-sized, golden cows of radiant colour, but trained to till the earth. Or they were medium-sized and golden, of radiant colour and did not till the earth, but they irrigated the fields.

They searched and searched and realized the evil of their bickering. 'What should she be like? What should her colour be? Where is she?' They grew weary.

Allah desired good for an orphan child and so they found this cow which Allah had described, and they had to pay him a very high price for it. *'They sacrificed it, but they almost did not do it.'* (2: 71)

Allah then commanded that the murdered man be struck with a piece of the cow. Then he came back to life and told them the name of his killer. That is indeed how it was.

The *Shari'a*

The Israelites left a life of beasts of burden for a life of men. They went to live in the desert as free and noble men. They needed a divine law to provide judgement between them and to illuminate a path for them. Mankind cannot live as human beings unless they have a divine law and a light from their Lord.

The entire world is darkness upon darkness except when someone has a shining light from his Lord; and that light is the light of the Prophets which gives people the guidance they need. Whoever is not guided by this light is astray and acts haphazardly. Without this light, beliefs are only fancies and superstitions for children to laugh at. *They only follow supposition and supposition does not help at all against the truth.* (53: 28) Have you not heard about the beliefs of polytheists, and other non-Muslims? Their knowledge is in fact ignorance, conjecture, superstition and hearsay. *They follow but a guess and lo! a guess can never take the place of the Truth.* (53: 28)

Their 'Morality' consists of nothing but excess and

negligence, laxity and prodigality. Do you not see how those who do not follow the Prophets violate people's rights, exceed the proper limits and follow their whims? Their government and politics are nothing but injustice, despotism and attacks on people's property, rights and lives.

Do you not see how the people in power who have no fear of Allah and do not follow the *Shari'a* break their trusts, abuse the property of Allah, and violate people's rights and lives? Do you not see how they enslave people and split them up into sects by slaughtering their men and letting their women live?

All the world is darkness within darkness within darkness except for the one who has a shining light from his Lord: *Shadows of darkness piled one upon another. When he puts forth his hand, he almost cannot see it. Whoever does not have a light assigned to him by Allah has no light.* (24: 40)

The Prophet teaches people how to worship Allah. He also teaches them how to behave with each other. The Prophet teaches people what is correct in life and what is correct in religion. He teaches them how to eat, how to drink, how to sleep, how to sit, how to behave in every situation.

The Prophet teaches people how to live as a kind father teaches his beloved children. People need the teaching of the Prophets as much, or even more than they needed the teaching of their parents when they were children.

Those who do not receive this prophetic teaching and do not learn manners from the Prophets are like wild trees. They grow up untended, so in them you see crookedness, thorniness and rottenness.

The Torah

Allah did not want the Israelites to perish as other nations, who had neither book nor guidance from Allah, had perished. He did not want them to act haphazardly as other nations had acted.

Allah commanded Musa to purify himself and to fast for thirty days. Then he was to go to Mount Sinai so that his Lord could speak to him and give him a book which would guide the Israelites. Musa picked out seventy men from his people to be witnesses to that because the Israelites were a contentious people.

Because the community must have a leader, *he said to his brother Harun: 'Be my successor among my people. Put things right. Do not follow the way of those who work corruption'* (7: 142)

Musa went to keep the appointment with his Lord, but his yearning drew him towards his Lord and he rushed ahead and arrived first at the Mount. Allah said, *'What has sped you ahead of your people, Musa?'*

He said, 'They are on my tracks. I have hastened to You, my Lord, only to please You.' (20: 83–4)

Allah commanded him to fulfil the appointment with his Lord by remaining forty days in all.

Musa went to Mount Sinai and his Lord spoke to him intimately and brought him near. This increased his yearning and he said: *'O my Lord, let me look at You!'* (7: 143)

Allah knew that this was not possible for Musa because *'the eyes do not perceive Him, but He does perceive the eyes. He is the Subtle, the Aware.'* (6: 103)

Even the mountains are unable to bear His words, let alone see Him: *'If We had sent down this Qur'an on a mountain, you would have seen it humbled, split asunder out of fear of Allah.'* (59: 21)

He said: 'You will not see Me, but look at the mountain. If it stays fast in its place, then you will see Me.' When his Lord revealed Himself to the mountain, He made it crumble to dust and Musa fell down in a swoon.

When he woke, he said: 'Glory be to Allah! I turn to You in repentance and I am the first of the believers.'

He said: 'Musa, I have chosen you over all the people for My message and My words. Take what I have given you and be one of the thankful.' (7: 144)

Musa took the Tablets which contained all the admonition that the Israelites needed and the details of everything. Allah commanded him to take hold of it forcefully and command his people to do their best according to it.

When Musa came to the seventy men of his people and told them what Allah had given him, they said insolently: *'We will not believe until we see Allah openly.'* (2: 55) Allah was angry at this impudence, so a thunderbolt struck them while they were looking. They realized that they could not even endure this thunderbolt which Allah had created. So how would they possibly be able to endure the light of Allah!

Musa called on his Lord and said: *'My Lord, if You had wished, You could have destroyed them before as well as me. Will You destroy us for what the foolish among us did?'* (7: 155)

Allah answered Musa's prayer and restored them to life so that they might show their gratitude.

The calf

The Israelites had lived with the idol-worshippers in Egypt for many generations. The Copts used to worship many things in Egypt. The Israelites had seen that with their own eyes. Dislike of idol-worship had slipped away from them and love of it had seeped into them, as water seeps into an old, unused house. Whenever they had the chance, they began to worship idols. Their hearts swerved and their tastes became corrupted. Whenever they saw the path of right guidance, they did not take it. Whenever they saw the path of error, they took it.

They crossed the sea and *came upon a people holding to idols they had. They said: 'Musa, make a god for us as they have gods.'*

Musa became angry and said, *'You are an ignorant people!* (7: 138–9)

'What unbelievable wickedness! Allah has blessed you and preferred you and given you what He has not given anyone else in the entire world! *Should I seek a god for you other than Allah who has preferred you over all beings?'* (7: 140)

When Musa went to the Mount and was absent from them for some days, they became playthings for Satan and fell prey to associating things with Allah. One of their men called 'the Samiri' got up *and produced a calf for them, a mere body that lowed. They said: 'This is your god and the god of Musa whom he has forgotten.'* (20: 88)

The Israelites were seduced by this calf and bowed to it, their hearts were so deaf and blind to truth. *What? Did they not see that that thing did not return any word to them nor possess power to harm or benefit them?* (20: 89) *Did they not see that it did not speak to them nor guide them upon a path?* (7: 148)

Harun forbade them to do this and tried hard to dissuade them, saying: *'O my people, you have been tempted by the thing. Your Lord is the All-Merciful. Follow me and obey what I command.'* (20: 90)

But the Israelites were seduced by the magic of the Samiri and love of the calf was made to sink into their hearts. They said: *'We will not cease to be its votaries until Musa returns to us.'* (20: 91)

The punishment

When Allah told Musa that the Samiri had misled the Israelites, he went back to his people in sorrow and anger. He was angry with his people and angry for Allah's sake with his brother Harun. He said: *'Harun, what kept you back, when you saw them going astray, that you did not follow me? Did you disobey my command?'*

Harun apologized and said: *'I was afraid that you would say, "You have divided the Children of Israel and have not observed my word."* (20: 92–4) *The people have abased me and nearly killed me.'* (7: 150)

He said: 'O my Lord, forgive me and my brother and admit us to Your mercy. You are the Most Merciful of the Merciful.' (7: 151)

Then Musa turned to the Samiri and said: *'What was your business, O Samiri?'*

The Samiri admitted his crime and said: *'That is how my self prompted me.'* (20: 96)

He said: 'Go! In this life it is for you to say, "Touch me not!"' (20: 97)

Musa punished him by isolating him. He had to walk alone and live alone like a wild creature without any friends. What punishment could be worse? The one who pollutes thousands of people with idol-worship should be considered unclean and shunned. The one who comes between Allah and His slaves should be separated from mankind. The one who calls people to idol-worship in the land of Allah is a great sinner, the entire earth should be his prison.

Then Musa commanded that the cursed calf should be burned. When that was done, he threw it into the sea. The Israelites saw the fate of the calf they had worshipped and saw that it was weak and powerless.

Musa turned to the Israelites and said: *'My people! You have wronged yourselves by taking the Calf. So turn to the Creator and kill yourselves. That would be better for you in your Creator's sight.'* (2: 54)

That is what they did. Those who had not worshipped the calf killed those who had worshipped it. So Allah turned to them.

Allah the Exalted said: *'Those who took the Calf will be overtaken by wrath from their Lord and abasement in the life of this world. That is how We repay forgers.'* (7: 152)

That is how calf-worshippers will be treated until the Day of Judgement! That is how all idol-worshippers and those who associate others with Allah will be treated until the Day of Judgement!

The cowardice of the Israelites

The Israelites had grown up in Egypt in slavery, humiliation and abasement. The children and the young men had only known this way of life. The blood had frozen in their veins. This was shown in their lack of courage, self-respect and enthusiasm. They were not used to leading

116

themselves, to struggling and fighting; they had never even talked about such matters.

Guided by revelation from Allah, Musa wanted them to enter the Holy Land. There they could live free and secure. But Musa recognized the cowardice and weakness in the character of the Israelites. He wanted to inspire them and to make things easy for them, for the Holy Land was controlled by a strong, arrogant people.

The Israelites refused to enter the Holy Land until those arrogant people had been driven from it. Musa mentioned Allah's blessing to them, how Allah had preferred them over all people, so that they would be eager to strive in the way of Allah and would despise the humiliating and undignified life they were leading.

When Musa said to his people, 'O my people, remember Allah's blessing to you, how He placed among you Prophets and made you kings and gave you what He did not give any of the people.' (5: 20)

Then he said to them: 'The Holy Land is before you. All you have to do is get up and take it from your enemies. When Allah wants and decrees something for someone, He makes it easy for him to have it. There is no averting the decree of Allah. *O my people, enter the Holy Land which Allah has ordained for you.'* He was afraid that their cowardice would get the better of them and added: *'Do not turn back on your backs for you will turn back as losers.'* (5: 21)

What Musa had been afraid of happened. Their answer, in spite of all that he had said, was: *'Musa, there are arrogant people in it. We will not enter it until they leave it. If they leave it, then we will enter.'* (5: 22)

Two men from among those who feared Allah, whom Allah had blessed, said: 'Enter the gate against them.

117

When you enter it, you will be the victors. Put your trust in Allah if you are believers.' (5: 23)

But that had no effect on them. They said: 'If it must be entered, then you enter it by means of a miracle. If we hear that you have entered it, then we will also come and enter in safety.'

They said: 'Musa, we will never enter it as long as they are in it. Go, you and your Lord and fight. We will remain sitting here.' (5: 24)

Then Musa became angry and despaired of those men. *He said: 'O my Lord, I have control of none but myself and my brother, so distinguish between us and the ungodly people.'*

Allah said: 'It will be forbidden to them for forty years while they wander in the land bewildered. Do not grieve for the ungodly people.' (5: 25)

During this period, the generation who had grown up in Egypt in servitude and abasement died. Another generation grew up who had been raised in this wandering, in hardship. That was the nation of the future. This has been the fate of the Jews in all times that they are a wandering nation leading a life of humiliation and slavery.

The path of knowledge

The Prophet Muhammad, may Allah bless him and grant him peace, said: 'Musa stood up to speak among the Israelites and was asked, "Who has the most knowledge?" He replied, "I have."'

Allah rebuked him for not having attributed all knowledge to Allah.

Allah revealed to him: 'One of My slaves who can be found at the place where the two seas meet knows more than you.'

118

He asked: 'O Lord, how can I find him?'

He was told: 'Carry a fish in a basket. When you lose it, he will be there.'

He set off with his servant, Yusha' ibn Nun. They carried a fish in a basket. They reached a rock, where they lay down and slept. The fish slipped out of the basket and made its way to the sea by burrowing. Musa and his servant witnessed this extraordinary happening.

They went on for the rest of the day and the following night. The next morning, Musa said to his servant: 'Bring us our breakfast. We have encountered weariness in this journey of ours.' Musa had not felt weary until he passed the place he had been commanded to reach.

His servant said: 'What do you think? When we took refuge in the rock, I forgot the fish.'

Musa said: 'That is what we were seeking.' So they turned back and retraced their steps.

When they reached the rock, they found a man wrapped in a cloak. Musa greeted him. The man, whose name was Al-Khadir, said, surprised: 'Is there such a greeting in your land?'

He said: 'I am Musa.'

He asked: 'Musa of the Israelites?'

Musa replied: 'Yes.' Then he asked: *Shall I follow you so that you can teach me right guidance from what you have been taught?'*

He said, 'You will not be able to bear with me patiently. (18: 66–7) Musa, I have some knowledge which Allah has taught me which He has not taught you. You have knowledge which Allah has taught you which I do not know.'

Musa said: *'If Allah wills, you will find me patient and I will not disobey you in anything.'* (18: 69)

119

They walked together beside the sea. They did not have a boat. Then a boat passed by and the people in it offered to carry them. Then the people recognized Al-Khadir and they carried them without charge.

A sparrow landed on the edge of the boat and pecked once or twice at the sea. Al-Khadir said: 'Musa, all that is lacking from my knowledge and your knowledge from Allah is like the pecking of this sparrow in the sea.'

Al-Khadir then stove in one of the panels of the boat. Musa said. 'These people have carried us for free and then you go and deliberately make a hole in their boat so that its people will drown!'

Al-Khadir said: *'Did I not say that you would not be able to bear with me patiently.'*

Musa said: *'Do not take me to task for forgetting and be not hard on me for my fault.'* (18: 73)

The first excuse given by Musa was that he had forgotten.

They went on until they came upon a boy playing with some other boys. Al-Khadir took hold of the top of the boy's head and jerked his head back with his hand. Musa said: *'What, have you killed an innocent soul who has slain no man?'*

He said: *'Did I not say to you that you would not be able to bear with me patiently?'* (18: 74–5)

They went on again until they came to a city. They asked the people there for food, but they refused to give them any. They found a wall in the city which was about to fall down. Al-Khadir set it upright with his own hand.

Musa said: *'If you had wished, you could have taken a wage for it.'*

He said: *'This is the parting between you and me.'* (18: 77–8)

The Prophet Muhammad, may Allah bless him and grant him peace, said: 'May Allah have mercy on Musa. We wish that he had been more patient so that we could have heard more about the two of them.' (Sahih al-Bukhari)

Interpretation

Then al-Khadir informed Musa: *'As for the boat, it belonged to some poor people who worked upon the sea. I wanted to damage it since there was a king behind them who was seizing every [sound] boat by force. (18: 79)*

'As for the boy, his parents were believers and we feared that he would grieve them with insolence and disbelief on them. We wanted for their Lord to give them a better one in purity and closer in affection. (18: 80–1)

'As for the wall, it belonged to two orphan boys in the city. There was a treasure under it which belonged to them. Their father was a righteous man so your Lord wanted for them to come of age and then bring forth their treasure as a mercy from your Lord. (18: 81)

'I did not do it of my own bidding. That is the interpretation of what you could not bear patiently.' (18: 82)

Then Musa realized that no-one could encompass all of Allah's knowledge and that some people have some of His knowledge while other people have another part of it. *Over everyone endowed with knowledge there is one more knowing.* (12: 76)

The Israelites after Musa

Musa died while the Israelites were still wandering in the land as a punishment from Allah and as a repayment for what they had done.

Allah afflicted them with abasement and poverty and they deserved His anger. They had angered Allah, the One who had appointed Prophets from among them and made them kings and had given them what He had not given any other people in their time.

Allah, the One Who had rescued them from the people of Pharaoh who were subjecting them to an evil punishment, slaughtering their sons and letting their daughters live.

Allah, the One Who had divided the sea for them and had rescued them and drowned the people of Pharaoh before their eyes.

Allah, the One Who had made the clouds shade them and had sent down *manna* and *salwa* for them.

Allah, the One Who had made the earth gush forth springs for them and had given them ample food and drink.

They repaid all that by rejecting the signs of Allah, rebelling and transgressing.

They angered their Prophet Musa, the kindest of Allah's creatures to them, the one who was kinder to them than their own fathers and mothers. He was as tender to them as a wet-nurse is to the baby she feeds, as a tender mother is towards her child.

The one they cursed, prayed for them. Whenever they laughed at him, he wept. Whenever they were harsh to him, he had pity on them.

He was the one who had rescued them from the tyrant Pharaoh and brought them out of Egypt to a land of freedom and honour, from a life of wretched slavery to a life of noble freedom.

They angered him, injured him, doggedly opposed him, mocked him, and considered him to be the humblest man among them while he was the most noble in the eyes of Allah.

Did they not deserve their punishment, wretchedness and constant wandering, and that they will never prosper? Yes, they indeed deserve all this and even worse because of their evil deeds: *'Allah did not wrong them. But they wronged themselves.'* (16: 33)

7. The Prophet Shu'ayb

To Midian, their brother Shu'ayb

In the Qur'an, is the story of the Prophet of Allah, Shu'ayb, whom He sent to Midian and the People of the Thicket. These people were merchants, and controlled the great trade routes between Yemen and Syria, and between Iraq and Egypt on the shores of the Red Sea.

They associated other gods with Allah as did the communities to whom other Prophets were sent in every age. Furthermore, they cheated in their dealings and gave short measure. Also, they interfered with the caravans and threatened and alarmed them. They caused havoc in the land, as people will who seek only power and riches in this life, and expect no reckoning nor fear any punishment in the Hereafter.

Allah sent His Messenger Shu'ayb to them to call them and warn them. He said to them: *'O my people, worship Allah. You have no god but Him. Do not diminish the measure and the balance. I see you are prosperous and I fear for you the punishment of an encompassing day.*

'O my people, fill up the balance and the measure justly and do not diminish the goods of the people and do not make havoc in the land, working corruption.' (11: 84–5)

124

Shu'ayb's call

Shu'ayb spoke to them at length and loosened the knot in their souls, the knot of love of poverty and worldly increase.

He said: 'The profit you receive after giving full measure and weight is better for you than taking people's property unjustly and through trickery. When you examine your life and the life of those who were wealthy and amassed riches, you will find that the actual result of everything they obtained through shortening, lessening and trickery was destruction, ruin, corruption and affliction. It was either stolen from them, or looted, or spent in ways which do not please Allah, or else someone gained control of it who wasted and squandered it. A small amount that brings true contentment is better than an abundance that does not.'

Say: 'The corrupt and the wholesome are not equal, even if the great amount of the corrupt pleases you.' (5: 100)

'My advice to you is pure and sincere. Allah alone is the One who watches over you.'

He spoke with compassion and wisdom, and from knowledge and insight: 'What remains with you from Allah is better for you if you are believers. I am not a guardian over you.' (11: 86)

A merciful father and a wise teacher

Shu'ayb spoke to them on many occasions and gave them advice as does any compassionate father and wise teacher.

He said: 'O my people, serve Allah! You have no god but Him. A clear sign has come to you from your Lord. So fill up the measure and the balance, and do not

125

diminish the goods of the people. Do not work corruption in the land after it has been set right. That is better for you if you are believers. Do not sit in every path, threatening and barring those who believe in Allah from the path of Allah, desiring to make it crooked. Remember when you were few and He multiplied you. See what was the end of those who worked corruption.' (7: 85–6)

His people's response

Those among Shu'ayb's people who were thought to be clever looked for bad motives in his words. They said in arrogant pride, as if they had discovered a secret or solved a riddle:

'Shu'ayb, does your prayer command you that we should abandon what our fathers worshipped or forbid us to do whatever we like with our own property? You are the forbearing, sensible.' (11: 87)

Shu'ayb explains his summons

Shu'ayb was kind to them, not harsh or angry. He told them that he had only taken it upon himself to deliver this summons and good counsel after a long time of bearing silently their corrupt morals and unjust behaviour. Then Allah had honoured him with prophethood and revelation, and opened his breast and given him a light from Him.

Envy was not the reason he spoke up. Allah had made him wealthy and given him wholesome, lawful provision. He was happy with that, cheerful and content, and thankful to Allah.

He did not forbid them from doing anything that he himself did, nor did he deny them anything that he himself indulged in. He was not one of those who command others to piety while they forget themselves, nor one of those who speak but do not act. He sought only to put them right, to direct them to contentment, and rescue them from the punishment which was hovering above their heads. All bounty returns to Allah and depends on Him.

He said: 'O my people, what do you think? If I stand upon a clear sign from my Lord, and He has given me an excellent provision from Him, and I do not desire to come behind you, taking myself to what I forbid you. I only desire to set things right as far as I can. My success is only with Allah. I have put my trust in Him and I turn to Him in repentance.' (11: 88)

We do not understand much of what you say

The people shut their ears to Shu'ayb's words. It was as if he were speaking to them in a foreign language, though he was one of them and from their own country. It was as if he was not making things clear, though he was both eloquent and clear in speech. But that is the way people are when they do not really want to accept good counsel.

Shu'ayb is amazed at his people

The people used Shu'ayb's weakness and isolation as an excuse. If it had not been for his tribe and kinsfolk, they would have stoned him and been rid of him. Shu'ayb was amazed that Allah, the All-Mighty, the All-Powerful, the All-Conquering, should be less in their eyes than a tribe which was subject to illness, weakness and destruction.

They said: 'Shu'ayb, we do not understand much of what you say. We see that you are weak among us. If

it had not been for your tribe, we would have stoned you.
You are not strong against us.'

He said: 'O my people, is my tribe stronger against
you than Allah? And have you taken Him as something to
thrust behind you? My Lord encompasses what you do.'
(11: 92)

The last bolt

When the people had finished their arguments, they
shot the last bolt which the arrogant of every nation shoot
against their Prophet and his followers. *The Council of*
those of his people said: 'Shu'ayb, we will drive you out
of our city along with those who believe with you unless
you return to our religion.' (7: 88)

A definitive proof

Shu'ayb's answer showed his pride in his faith and
his way of life, his earnest concern for his belief. When
they urged him to return to their religion, he said:
'Even though we detest it? We would have forged
lies against Allah if we were to return to your religion after
Allah has saved us from it. It is not for us to return to it
unless Allah our Lord wills. Our Lord encompasses all
things in His knowledge. In Allah we put all our trust. Our
Lord, decide with truth between us and our people. You
are the best of those who make decisions.'

They said the same as those before them said

The people responded the same as those before
them had responded: *They said: 'You are one of the*

bewitched. You are only a mortal like us. Indeed, we think that you are one of the liars. Cause lumps to fall on us from heaven if you are one of the truthful.' (26: 187)

The end of a nation who rejected their Prophet

Their end was the same as that of every community which rejects its Prophet and is ungrateful for the blessing of Allah. *So the earthquake seized them, and morning found them prostrate in their dwellings. Those who cried lies to Shu'ayb, it was as if they had never lived there. Those who cried lies to Shu'ayb were the losers.* (7: 92)

He conveyed the message and discharged the trust

Shu'ayb, like all the Prophets, delivered the message of Allah to his people, fulfilling the task entrusted to him, and he established the proof of it.

He turned his back on them and said: 'O my people, I have conveyed to you the messages of my Lord and I have given you good counsel. Why then should I grieve for an unbelieving people?' (7: 93)

8. The Prophets Da'ud and Sulayman

The Qur'an records the rejection, humiliation and banishment which the Prophets and Messengers suffered at the hands of the communities to which they were sent. It also mentions the punishment, the destruction and ruin that came upon these communities when they rejected their Messengers, mocked them, and conspired against their lives, as you have read in the stories of the Prophets we have already recounted.

The Qur'an mentions Allah's blessings

The Qur'an frequently mentions Allah's blessings and speaks, sometimes at length and sometimes briefly, about the numerous blessings which He conferred on many of the Prophets, including Da'ud, Sulayman, Ayyub, Yunus, Zakariyya and Yahya.

Allah made Da'ud and Sulayman strong in their land and gave them a great kingdom. He gave them knowledge, teaching them many things which other people did not know. Strong and insolent men and animals and objects that were not easy to deal with were subjected to them.

He said: 'We gave Da'ud and Sulayman knowledge.' They said: 'Praise belongs to Allah who has *preferred us over many of His believing slaves.' Sulayman was Da'ud's heir and said: 'People, we have been taught the speech of birds and we have been given abundance of every thing. This is the clear bounty.'* (27: 16)

Allah's blessing to Da'ud

As for Da'ud, Allah subjected to him the mountains and the birds, which echoed His praises and answered him in glorious song. He taught him the craft of making coats of mail and made ironwork easy for him. *We gave Da'ud bounty from Us: 'O mountains! Echo Allah's praises with him, and you birds.' We made iron soft for him. 'Fashion coats of mail and measure the links well. Act righteously. I see what you do.'* (34: 10)

And He also says: *'We subjected the mountains with Da'ud to glorify, and the birds, and We were the Doer. We taught him the craft of fashioning garments for you to protect you against your violence. Will you then not be thankful?'* (21: 79–80)

His gratitude for this blessing

Although Da'ud owned a wide kingdom with power and authority that he used well, he was still a humble, penitent slave of Allah. He constantly remembered Allah and spent long periods praying to Him and glorifying Him. He was a just ruler and an impartial judge who gave judgement between people according to the truth. Allah says: *'O Da'ud, We have made you a successor (khalifa) in the land, so judge between people according to the truth. Do not follow caprice so that it leads you astray from the way of Allah. Those who go astray from the way of*

131

Allah will have a harsh punishment for that they forgot the Day of Reckoning.' (38: 26)

Allah's blessing upon Sulayman

To Sulayman Allah subjected the winds. They blew at his command and carried him from place to place so that he reached his destination quickly. Allah also subjected to him the strong and clever *jinn* and the rebellious satans. They obeyed his commands and carried out his construction plans:

And to Sulayman the wind, blowing strongly, that ran at his command to the land which We had blessed. And We had knowledge of everything. Some of the satans dived for him (for pearls) and did other work as well; and We were watching over them. (21: 81–2)

And to Sulayman the wind, its morning course was a month's journey and its evening course was a month's journey. We made the fount of molten brass to flow for him. Some of the jinn worked for him by the leave of his Lord, and such of them as deviated from Our command We caused them to taste the punishment of the Blazing Fire. They made for him whatever he wanted: places of worship, statues, great pots like water-troughs and boilers built into the ground. 'Work, House of Da'ud, in thankfulness. Very few of My slaves are thankful.' (34: 12)

Fine understanding and deep knowledge

Sulayman's intelligence and sound judgement was shown in a case which was presented before his noble father. There was a vineyard full of grape-vines which were full of grapes. Some sheep belonging to another person entered the vineyard and ruined it. Da'ud gave a judgement that the sheep should be given to the owner of the vines in compensation. Sulayman said: 'That is not the more correct judgement, O Prophet of Allah.' Da'ud asked: 'What should it be then?' Sulayman said: 'Give the vines to the owner of the sheep and let him restore them to their previous condition. Give the sheep to the owner of the vines and he can profit from them until the vines are restored to their proper condition. Then the vines will be returned to their owner and the sheep will be returned to their owner.'

Allah gave him fine understanding and deep knowledge. Allah said: *'And Da'ud and Sulayman when they gave judgement concerning the fields, when the sheep of the people strayed there, and We were witnesses to their judgement. We made Sulayman understand it. We gave both of them judgement and knowledge.'* (21: 78–9)

Sulayman knew the language of the birds and animals

The Qur'an tells a delightful story which illustrates Sulayman's wisdom in the management of his kingdom and his awesome power. It shows how Allah joined for him the happiness of this world and the Next World. With Sulayman, his kingdom in this world strengthened his work as Prophet and Messenger of the true religion.

Sulayman knew the language of birds and animals. Once he mustered his armies of *jinn,* men and birds and rode among them in splendour and might. They were perfectly organized and arranged under the command of their leaders. Sulayman passed by the Valley of the Ants. One of the ants, afraid that the hooves of the horses would crush his tribe without Sulayman and his armies being aware of it, ordered his fellow-ants to go into their dwelling-places. Sulayman heard and understood this. Being a Prophet of Allah, his response was not ruled by pride or arrogance. Rather, Sulayman was moved to praise Allah and to be grateful for His blessing. Supplication and success are part of right action and treading in the path of the righteous slaves of Allah.

The story of the hoopoe

The hoopoe was Sulayman's scout and his eyes to seek out for him watering places and camp sites for the army. On one occasion, Sulayman could not locate the bird and this annoyed him. The hoopoe was away for quite a time before finally returning with this news for Sulayman: 'I have learned something that neither you nor your armies know. I have brought you true information about the kingdom of Sheba. It is a great and a vast state. But in spite of the intelligence and skill of the people, and their good leadership, I found them to be ignorant and foolish. They prostrate to the sun instead of Allah. They have no understanding and will not be guided to the worship of Allah alone.'

Sulayman calls the Queen of Sheba to true religion

It grieved the Prophet of Allah to learn of such a kingdom, with a people he had not known about. His call had not been able to reach these people so they still worshipped the sun. The zeal of Prophethood moved him to write to their idol-worshipping Queen, calling her to Islam and submission, before he advanced with his powerful armies to conquer her land. He wrote her an eloquent

134

letter in which he called on her to enter Islam and submit to him. The letter, which was polite but firm, expressed prophetic humility as well as kingly honour.

The Queen consults the leaders of her kingdom

The Queen of Sheba was intelligent and not given to hasty judgements. She had great experience of the conduct of kings and the history of conquerors. However, her intellect had deceived her as she had failed to recognize Allah and worship Him. She told her most intelligent counsellors that she had received a letter, different from all other letters. It was from the greatest king of that time who was a Prophet calling people to Allah. She asked for their advice.

The leaders in her kingdom began to vaunt their strength and the size of their armies. That is what companions of kings and rulers do in every time and place. The Queen did not agree with what they were doing, so they left the decision to her. She warned them about coming to a bad end. She reminded them how victorious kings despoil nations they have conquered, and humiliate even the noblest of people. She told them: 'I will send him some splendid gifts in order to test him. If he accepts the gifts, then he is a king and we will fight against him. If he does not accept them, then he is a Prophet and we will follow him.'

A bargained gift

She sent a delegation with gifts of great value as befits a king. When the gifts reached Sulayman, he refused to accept them, saying: 'Are you trying to use wealth to bargain with me so that I should leave you to hold your kingdom and your people in idol-worship? The kingdom, property and armies that Allah has given me are better than those you have. This is no light matter, but a serious and solemn call to true religion. It is a case of being summoned and of submitting, and not to be haggled over.' He sent the delegation back, declaring that he would march against their kingdom.

The Queen comes in submission

When the delegation returned to the kingdom of Sheba and gave the Queen Sulayman's message, she and her people decided they should obey. In submission she set out to meet Sulayman with her armies. When Sulayman learned of the decision, he was pleased and praised Allah. He wanted to show her a sign to illustrate the power of Allah and His blessings to Sulayman. He decided to present her with her own throne which was guarded by her strong, trustworthy men. He asked his Council to bring her throne to him before the Queen's great retinue arrived.

The throne was brought miraculously to Sulayman in the shortest possible time. Then, Sulayman commanded some of the finer details of the throne to be altered so that he could test whether the Queen would recognize it when she saw it. If she did not recognize it, that would prove that she was short-sighted in still finer matters that are even more difficult to grasp.

A great pavilion of glass

Sulayman commanded his builders, both *jinn* and men, to build a great pavilion with water flowing under a glass floor. Anyone who did not know the truth of the matter would have thought that they were really stepping into water. The Queen would surely assume that it was water and raise the hem of her dress above the water, and her mistake would be clear. She would then realize that she was short-sighted and had been deceived by outward appearances. She and her people were bowing to the sun because it was the clearest source of light and life, which are but two of Allah's attributes. Then the veil would fall from her eyes and she would realize that just as she had made a mistake in assuming the glass to be water when she raised the hem of her dress, so too she had been mistaken when she treated the sun as the Creator by prostrating to it and worshipping it.

The Queen surrenders with Sulayman to Allah, the Lord of all the worlds

All of that indeed happened. The Queen fell into this absurd error in spite of her cleverness. She thought that the glass was flowing, glistening water. She raised the hem of her dress above what she thought was the water.

Then the Prophet of Allah, Sulayman, informed her of her mistake, saying: 'It is a pavilion paved with crystal.' The veil fell from her eyes and she recognized her ignorance in taking an outward appearance at face value by worshipping the sun and prostrating to it. She was quick to exclaim: 'My Lord, I have wronged myself! I surrender with Sulayman to Allah, the Lord of all being.'

The Qur'an tells the story of Sulayman

Read this splendid, delightful story in the Qur'an. Allah says:

He searched among the birds. Then he said: 'How is it that I do not see the hoopoe? Or is he one of the absent? I will punish him with a harsh punishment or I will slaughter him or he will bring me a good reason.' But he did not delay long. He said: 'I have learned what you do not know. I have brought you sure news from Sheba. I found a woman ruling over them and she has been given some of everything and she has an immense throne. I found her and her people prostrating to the sun instead of Allah. Satan has made their actions seem fair to them and has barred them from the way. They are not guided, so they do not prostrate to Allah who brings forth what is hidden in the heavens and the earth. He knows what you conceal and what you make known. There is no god but Him, the Lord of the Immense Throne.'

He said: 'We will see if you have spoken the truth or whether you are one of the liars. Take this letter of mine and throw it to them. Then turn back from them and see how they return.'

She said: 'O Council! a noble letter has been cast to me. It is from Sulayman. It says: "In the name of Allah, the Merciful, the Compassionate. Do not rise up against me, but come to me in surrender." She said: 'O Council, give me your opinion in my affair. I am not in the habit of taking a firm decision in an affair until you bear witness to me.'

They said: 'We possess power and great might. The affair is up to you. Consider what command you will give.'

She said: 'When kings enter a city, they lay waste to it and make its mighty people abased. They will behave like that. I will send them a gift and see what answer the messengers bring back.'

When he came to Sulayman, he (Sulayman) said: 'What, would you assist me with wealth when what Allah *has given me is better than what He has given you? No, you delight in your gift! Go back to them. We will come against them with armies which they cannot resist and we will drive them out of there, abased and utterly humbled.'*

He said: 'O Council, which of you can bring me her throne before they come to me in surrender?' A powerful one of the jinn *said: 'I will bring it to you before you rise from your seat. I have the strength to do that and I am trustworthy.' The one who had knowledge of the Book said: 'I will bring it to you before your glance returns to you.'*

When he saw it settled before him, he said: 'This is part of the bounty of my Lord in order to test me to see whether I will be thankful or ungrateful. Whoever gives thanks, gives thanks for himself. Whoever is ungrateful, my Lord is Rich, Generous.' He said: 'Disguise her throne for her. We will see if she is guided or if she is one of those who are not guided.'

When she came, it was said: 'Is your throne like that?' She said: 'It is as though the very same.' 'We were given the knowledge before her and we were in surrender, but what she worshipped instead of Allah prevented her (understanding) or she was one of the people who disbelieve.' She was told: 'Enter the pavilion.' When she saw it, she supposed that it was open water and bared her legs. He said: 'It is a pavilion covered with crystal.' She said: 'I have wronged myself. I surrender with Sulayman to Allah, the Lord of all the worlds.' (27: 20–44)

This was what the Prophet of Allah, Sulayman, was like. He stood firm in his call for the Oneness of Allah. He had wisdom, understanding, and strong zeal for the true religion and its purity.

Sulayman believed, but the Satans did not believe

Yet the Jews attributed to Sulayman, sorcery, disbelief, and compromise with idol-worship. They even said that his wives had been able to weaken his belief in the unity of Allah. But Allah has declared that he was innocent of all these things.

Allah said: *'Sulayman did not unbelieve. The satans unbelieved and taught people magic.'* (38: 30) And: *'We gave to Da'ud, Sulayman. What an excellent servant he was! He was penitent.'* And: *'He had a near place in Our presence and an excellent return.'* (38: 40)

9. The Prophets Ayyub and Yunus

The story of Ayyub

The story of the Prophet Ayyub in the Qur'an shows another aspect of the blessing of Allah to His believing slaves who remain patient and thankful, and to His beloved Prophets.

Ayyub had many animals, flocks and fields, and fine sons, with all of whom he was pleased. He was put to the test regarding all these things and lost them all. Then he was put to the test regarding his own body until none of it was left healthy and sound, except for his heart and his tongue with which he remembered Allah. He was alone in a far-away corner of the land. No-one felt any pity for him except his wife who looked after him. They were in such need that she had to work as a servant.

Ayyub's patience

In spite of all this, Ayyub remained steadfast in his patience. He was constantly remembering and thanking Allah. He did not complain nor apportion blame nor grumble nor get angry. He remained in this state for several years.

Affliction and gift

When the affliction Allah had willed for Ayyub's soul was over he was allowed to be at peace. Allah inspired him with a supplication that was answered. That prayer revealed and expressed his powerlessness and misery. It revealed that there is indeed no refuge from Allah except in Him, and that He has the power to do anything. Allah healed Ayyub's body and restored his family and property to him, and blessed him. Allah says:

When Ayyub called unto his Lord: 'Affliction has visited me and You are the Most Merciful of the Merciful', We answered him and removed the affliction that was on him, and We gave him family and the like of them with them as a mercy from Us and a reminder to the slaves.' (21: 83)

The story of Yunus and its wisdom

The story of Yunus is linked to the story of Ayyub. Once again it affirms Allah's power, His kindness to His slaves and His help for them when they are in despair. When hope has gone and death approaches to crush the delicate stem of life, the Hand of Divine Power is found to be strong, and merciful.

Yunus among his people

Allah sent Yunus to the people of the village of Nineveh. He called them to Allah but they rejected him and were stubborn in their unbelief. Angrily, he left them, promising them that they would be punished after three days. Knowing that Prophets do not lie, the people of Nineveh took heed and went out into the desert with their children, cattle and flocks. There they humbly entreated Allah and prayed fervently to Him. The camels and their young grumbled; the cows and calves lowed; the sheep and lambs bleated. So Allah removed the punishment from them.

Why was there never a city that believed, and its belief profited it? Except for the people of Yunus. When they believed, We removed the punishment of disgrace from them in the life of this world and We gave them enjoyment for a time. (10: 98)

Yunus inside the belly of the fish

As for Yunus, he had embarked on a ship with some other people. It ran aground and, as they were afraid of drowning, they drew lots to decide which of the men they should throw overboard to lighten the ship. The lot fell on Yunus, but they refused to throw him overboard. They did it again and the lot again fell on him, but they still refused to do it. Then they did it a third time and again the lot fell on Yunus. Allah said: *'He cast lots and was one of the refuted'* (37: 41)

Yunus then got up and threw himself into the sea. Allah, glory be to Him!, sent a fish to him. When he jumped into the water the fish swallowed him. Allah revealed to the fish not to eat the flesh nor break the bones of Yunus.

Allah answers his supplication

Yunus was in darkness in the belly of the fish in the darkness of the sea in the darkness of the night. Many darknesses, one within the other! What intense darkness! How far away safety was! He remained there for as long as Allah willed. Then Allah inspired him to disperse the darkness, remove his distress and to call down mercy from above the seven heavens. The Qur'an recounts this unique and strange story which contains solace for all who are in misery and despair. They can see that there is no shelter from Allah except in Allah:

When Dhu'n-Nun left in anger and thought that We would have no power over him. Then he called out in the darknesses: 'There is no god but You! Glory be to You! I am one of the wrong-doers.' We answered him and We rescued him from grief. That is how We rescue the believers. (21: 87)

10. The Prophets Zakariyya and Yahya

Zakariyya's prayer for a righteous son

Another way in which Allah blesses His slaves, and reveals a sign of His power that encompasses all things, is found in the prayer of Zakariyya. Zakariyya prayed for a son who would be righteous, pleasing to Allah, dutiful and God-fearing; who would be his heir in the line of Ya'qub, of the great family of Prophets who called people to worship Allah. When Zakariyya prayed for a son, he was so advanced in years that his bones were weak and his hair was white. He had lost any hope that his wife could ever bear a child.

Yet, Allah answered his prayer. He gave him a right-guided son. While this child was still young, Allah granted him excellence, wisdom, forbearance, and knowledge, and He bestowed upon him the Book. The boy was endowed with compassion, righteousness, *taqwa* (piety), and obedience towards his parents. From his compassion the virtues of kindness, gentleness and humility flowed.

Allah fortified Zakariyya's heart and showed him signs of His infinite power to do whatever He wills and to create whatever He wills. Allah showed Zakariyya in person how He can act in His creation. Zakariyya understood that Allah can make possible what He wills. All existence is under His command: He brings forth the living from the dead, and brings forth the dead from the living, and provides for whomever He likes without reckoning.

The vow of 'Imran's wife

'Imran's wife was of the family of the Prophet Zakariyya. She was a righteous woman who loved Allah and His true religion. She had vowed that if she gave birth to a boy, she would give this child to Allah to serve His religion. She asked Allah to accept this child, to help His religion and His servants through him, and to make him one of the Imams of guidance who call to Allah.

She said: 'My Lord, I have given birth to a girl'

This righteous woman wanted one thing but Allah had willed another. Allah has the best knowledge of what is best for His servants. She gave birth to a girl. She became sad and depressed. But this girl was not like other girls. She was stronger in worship and had more zeal for acts of obedience and good deeds than many boys. When Allah decreed, by a wisdom that only He knew, that the child should be a girl, He also decreed that she should be the mother of a righteous Prophet of great importance, for the burdens of prophethood are only taken on by men.

When the wife of 'Imran said: 'Lord, I have vowed that what is in my womb will belong to You and be devoted to Your service. Accept this from me. You are the Hearing, the Knowing.' When she gave birth to her, she said: 'Lord, I have given birth to her, a girl.' Allah knew better what she had given birth to. The male is not like the female. 'I have named her Maryam and I have entrusted her to You

146

to protect her and her children from the accursed Satan.'
(3: 35–6)

Allah's care for the righteous girl

The girl was put in the care of Zakariyya because of her relationship to him. She was also in the care of Allah who, as Zakariyya saw, gave her fruits outside of their proper season and place. She ate what she liked of them and gave away whatever she wished.

Her Lord accepted her with favour, and made her grow up well and beautiful. Zakariyya assumed the responsibility for her. Whenever Zakariyya came to her in the inner sanctuary, he found that she had food. He said: 'Maryam, how did you get this?' She said: 'It is from Allah. Allah provides for whomever He will without reckoning.' (3: 36)

An inspiration from the Merciful Lord

Thus Allah revealed to Zakariyya, one of the Prophets and a wise, intelligent man, that the One who could give fruits out of their season to a righteous girl was well able to give a son to an old man advanced in age, even when he had given up hope owing to his great age and his wife's barrenness.

Zakariyya's hopes and aspirations were revived. His spirit soared, and his trust in his Lord was strong. His tongue poured forth supplication which the angels were entrusted with and which set in motion the mercy of Allah. That was an inspiration from the Merciful Lord and something decreed by the All-Mighty, the All-Knowing.

There Zakariyya called on his Lord, saying: 'My Lord, give me good offspring from You. You are the One who hears the supplication.' (3: 38)

Good news of a son

Allah answered his prayer and sent him the good news of a righteous son soon to be born.

Man was created hasty. Zakariyya asked for a sign of this great event and how near it was. *He said: 'My Lord, give me a sign.'*

He said: 'Your sign is that you will not speak to people for three days except by gestures. Remember your Lord often and glorify Him in evenings and mornings.' (3: 41)

Allah can make the articulate tongue dumb, unable to utter a single word. He can endow whatever creatures He wills with whatever properties He wills.

The signs of Allah and His power

The signs of Allah and His power were evident in Zakariyya's body, and his house and family. Yahya was born. He delighted Zakariyya, assisted him and kept his mission alive.

The Qur'an says: *And Zakariyya, when he called unto his Lord: 'O my Lord, do not leave me alone. You are the best of inheritors.' We answered him, and gave him Yahya and We set his wife right for him. They vied with each other, hastening to good works and called to Us in yearning and awe. They were humble to Us.* (21: 89–90)

Yahya takes on the burden of the call

Yahya was a delight to his parents and a successor to his noble father. He took on the burden of calling to Allah and the pure religion. He had a great passion for knowledge when he was still a boy and he was endowed with righteousness and *taqwa* even as a young man. He surpassed his comrades in love, compassion, and obedience to his parents so that people would point him out. Allah says when He addresses him: *'O Yahya, take the Book with force.' We gave him judgement as a child, and tenderness and purity from Us. He was God-fearing and dutiful to his parents, not arrogant and rebellious. 'Peace be upon him the day he was born, the day he dies and the day when he will be raised up alive!'* (19: 12–15)

11. The Prophet 'Isa ibn Maryam

The story of a miracle

The Prophet 'Isa was the last of the Messengers before the Prophet Muhammad, may Allah bless him and grant him peace. His is a story which reveals the conquering Will of Allah, His absolute Power and His fine Wisdom. Everything about 'Isa is a miracle. His birth was such a miracle that it is hard to believe in. People who reject Allah believe only in what they can see for themselves. They are ignorant of the Power of Allah which controls all things, and of the Will of Allah which cannot be resisted. *His command when He wills something is that He says, 'Be!' and it is.* (36: 82)

However, the birth of 'Isa is accepted easily by those who believe in Allah as a powerful, transforming God, a Creator and a Maker. *He is Allah, the Creator, the Maker, the Fashioner. He has the most beautiful names. All that is in the heavens and the earth glorifies Him. He is the Mighty, the Wise.* (59: 24)

Such people believe that Adam was created from water and clay without a mother or father. To believe in a birth by a mother without a father is easier than to believe in a birth without a mother or a father. That is why Allah said: *The similitude of Jesus before God is as that of Adam.*

He created him from earth and then said to him, 'Be!' and he was. (3: 59)

Everything about 'Isa was extraordinary

Everything related to the Prophet 'Isa was extraordinary. He was born at a time when Greece had made its greatest advances in rational sciences, mathematics and medicine.

The Jews followed a worldly point of view

The Jews, though a community who had given many Prophets, at this time rejected the Spirit of God and anything connected to it. They found a worldly explanation for everything. The miracles which Allah bestowed on the Prophet 'Isa were designed to cure that narrow, worldly point of view. It was what was needed in that age.

As a community, the Jews depended only on what they themselves witnessed. They had a great veneration for race and blood, and a love of money and property. They were completely engrossed in this life. Their hearts became hard, and their natures became course. They were not kind to the weak nor gentle towards the poor. They treated people who had no Israelite blood in their veins as worthless. They were humble towards the strong and rich, and tyrannical towards the poor and weak. They were harsh when they had power and yielding when they were without power. Hypocrisy and servility, trickery and cunning, and resorting to conspiracy and secretiveness were engendered in them by a life of abasement and servitude which they had long endured in Syria and Palestine under Roman rule.

151

Scorn and disobedience

Over the ages, the Jews' scorn for the Prophets had increased. So too, in their community, had murder, dealings with usury, joking about religious teachings, and lack of compassion. The hearts of many of them were stripped of sincere love of Allah. They forgot about charity, equality, piety and generosity. They had once believed in Prophethood and the Message, and there had been many Prophets among them and their books were filled with reports about them. But, in the end, they only believed in what suited their purpose. They opposed those who criticized them, called them to account and called them to true religion, and even made war on them.

Allah's blessing to the Israelites

At one time the Jews had been a nation apart from other nations by their belief in the Divine Unity. That is why they were preferred over other people at that time. Allah the Exalted says: *'O Children of Israel, remember My blessing to you which I bestowed on you and that I preferred you over all the worlds.'* (2: 47)

Ingratitude

Because they mixed with idol-worshipping people, gradually the Jews failed to honour the teachings of the Prophets. They began to adopt spurious beliefs and ignorant customs. They had worshipped the Calf after their escape from Egypt, and they developed a great veneration for 'Uzayr, even claiming that he was more than human. Their insolence led them to ascribe idol-worship, magic and unbelief and ugly deeds to certain Prophets. They did not fear Allah any more.

Pride and conceit

In spite of all these faults, the Jews took great pride in their lineage and gave great weight to their hopes and dreams. They said: *'We are the sons and beloved of Allah.'* (5: 18) And they said: *'The Fire will only touch us for a certain number of days.'* (2: 80)

The birth of the Messiah challenges the ordinary senses

The birth, life, and message of the Messiah challenged the Jews' perception, custom and law. It also challenged the highest ideals in which they believed and the ends for which they competed and fought. The Messiah was born in a most unusual way. He spoke to people while he was still in the cradle and grew up in the care of a poor, chaste mother. He lived in a climate of slander and hostility, far from the trappings of prestige and wealth. He sat with poor people, ate with them and was kind to them. He comforted the weak and the stranger. He treated equally the rich and the poor, the judge and the judged, and the high-born and the lowly.

The miracles of the Messiah

Allah granted the Messiah Prophethood and revelation. He gave him the Gospel and supported him with the Holy Spirit and wonderful miracles. Allah gave him healing for the sick whom the doctors had failed to cure. He healed people who had been blind from birth, and the lepers, and brought the dead to life by the permission of Allah. He shaped clay into something like the form of a bird, and then breathed into it and it became a bird by the permission of Allah. He told people what they had eaten and what they had stored up in their houses.

All of this restored trust and belief in the miracles of the Messengers and the reports of divine power contained in the Torah. But those who rejected the reality of Divine Power and the force of the Will of the Lord rose up. They declared that there could be nothing new and nothing beyond the worldly knowledge they already possessed.

'Isa's call to true religion and the Jews' rejection of him

'Isa uncovered the lies of the Jews in many of the matters that they had dreamed up and practised. They made unlawful what Allah had made lawful and lawful what Allah had made unlawful. 'Isa began to call them to the spirit and heart of true religion, to its basis and inward reality, to the love of Allah which comes before every other love, to mercy and respect for mankind, and to charity towards the poor. He called them to pure belief in God and dismissed all the ignorant customs and false beliefs which had crept into the religion of the Prophets.

The Jews oppose 'Isa

Isa's teaching proved unbearable to the Jews. They became hostile to him. They poured blame on him, and taunted him with suspicions and slander. They used curses and foul words against him. They slandered his mother, Maryam the Virgin. They attacked him, aroused the rabble against him and ridiculed his teachings.

The story of 'Isa in the Qur'an

Then the Jews sought to kill 'Isa and be rid of him, but Allah protected him and turned their plots back against them. He raised him to Himself and honoured him. Read the story in the Qur'an:

When the angels said: 'Maryam! Allah gives you the good news of a word from Him. His name is Messiah, 'Isa the son of Maryam, noteworthy in this world and in the Hereafter, one of those brought near. He will speak to people in the cradle and when he is an adult. He is one of the righteous.'

She said: 'My Lord! How can I have a son when no man has touched me?' He said: 'Just like that. Allah creates whatever He wills. When He decrees something, He only says to it, "Be!" and it is. He will teach him the Book, the Wisdom, the Torah and the Gospel, and he will be a Messenger to the Children of Israel.'

'I have brought you a sign from your Lord. I will form for you out of clay something similar to the form of a bird and I will breathe into it and it will become a bird by Allah's permission. I will heal the blind from birth and the leper and I will bring the dead back to life by the permission of Allah and tell you what you eat and what you store up in your houses. There is a sign for you in that if you are believers. I confirm what is before me of the Torah and to make lawful for you some of what was unlawful for you. I have brought you a sign from your Lord. So fear Allah and obey me. Allah is my Lord and your Lord, so worship Him. This is a straight path.'

When 'Isa sensed rejection in them, he said: 'Who are my helpers to Allah?' The disciples said: 'We are the helpers of Allah. We believe in Allah. We testify that we are those who submit (to Him). Our Lord, we believe in what You have sent down. We follow the Messenger, so write us down among the witnesses!' (Those who rejected) plotted and Allah plotted. Allah is the best of plotters.

155

When Allah said: "'Isa, I will take you and raise you up to Me and purify you from those who have rejected. I will place those who follow you above those who have rejected until the Day of Judgement. Then you (all) will return to Me and I will judge between you regarding that about which you used to differ. Those who reject, I will punish them with a terrible punishment in this world and the Next World. They will have no helpers.'

Those who believe and do good deeds will be given their wages in full. Allah does not love the wrong-doers. That is what We recite to you of the signs and Wise Reminder.

The example of 'Isa in the sight of Allah is as the example of Adam. He created him from earth and then He said to him, 'Be!' and he was. The truth is from your Lord. Do not be one of the doubters.' (3: 45–60)

'Isa's life and call in the Qur'an

Read Allah's description of 'Isa's life and call:

'I am the slave of Allah. Allah has given me the Book and made me a Prophet. He has made me blessed wherever I am and has enjoined me to pray and to pay the zakat as long as I am alive and to be dutiful to my mother. He did not make me arrogant and wretched. Peace be upon me the day I was born, the day I die and the day I will be raised up alive.' (19: 30–3)

An eternal conflict

What had happened to other Prophets before him happened to 'Isa. The rulers and leaders kept away from him. The rich and powerful ignored him. They thought it a sin to believe in him and his followers. They would not give up the leadership, position, privilege and distinction they enjoyed. The words of Allah are true:

We sent no warner into any city except that its wealthy said: 'We disbelieve in the Message you have been sent with.' They also said: 'We are more abundant in wealth and children, and we will not be punished.' (34: 34–5)

The belief of the common and poor people

'Isa despaired of the obstinacy and disbelief of the wealthy people. They rejected the clear signs and wonderful miracles he had brought even though they knew they were true. They belittled him because he did not have power and might. So 'Isa devoted himself to the common and poor people whose hearts yielded, whose souls were pure because they lived by the toil of their hands and the sweat of their brows. They did not boast of lineage nor become insolent because of rank and position. A group of them, including fishermen, craftsmen and workers believed.

We are the helpers of Allah

These people believed in the Messiah and gathered around him and placed their hands in his hand and said: *'We are the helpers of Allah.'* Allah says:

When 'Isa sensed rejection in them, he said: 'Who are my helpers to Allah?' The disciples said: 'We are the helpers of Allah. We believe in Allah. We testify that we are those who submit (to Him). Our Lord, we believe in what You have sent down. We follow the Messenger, so write us down among the witnesses!' (3: 52–3)

Travel and call

'Isa spent most of his time travelling from place to place teaching about the One God. He called the Israelites to Allah and guided those among them who were astray to their Lord and Master. In his travels he met with both ease and hardship. He endured all this with patience and accepted it in gratitude. He endured hunger and was content with just enough food to keep body and soul together.

The disciples ask for a table from heaven

The disciples did not have the same degree of patience that 'Isa had, not his steadfastness, discipline and self-control. They were afflicted by the continual hardship and wanted 'Isa to ask Allah to send down a table from heaven for them, from which they could eat and be filled after their hunger, and have comfort after their difficulties.

Improper manners

But the disciples did not behave correctly when making their request. They said: *'Is it possible for your Lord to send down on us a Table from out of heaven?'* (5: 112) 'Isa did not like their request or the manner in which they presented it to him. The Prophets ask their communities to believe in the Unseen, and make it obligatory for them to do so. Miracles are not games to amuse children and divert the gullible. They are signs from Allah which He manifests at the hands of His Prophets whenever He likes. Through them the proof of Allah is established against His slaves. They are not given any reprieve after these miracles appear and are rejected.

Warning his people about a bad punishment

'Isa was afraid for the disciples because of their request for a table from heaven. He warned them about incurring an evil punishment. He forbade them to put Allah to the test. He is too High and Majestic for that.

Insistence and earnest request

But the disciples repeated their request. They explained that they did not intend to test Allah, rather they wanted to put their hearts at ease. They intended it to be a reminder to future generations and a story to be told and reported for years to come. It would be a proof of the truth of the religion and of the situation of the first believers and truthful disciples.

The Qur'an relates the story

The Qur'an recounts this story thus:

When the disciples said: 'O 'Isa son of Maryam, is it possible for your Lord to send down on us a Table from out of heaven?' He said: 'Fear Allah, if you are believers.' They said: 'We want to eat from it and for our hearts to be at rest, and that we may know that you have spoken the truth to us, and that we may be among the witnesses to that.' 'Isa the son of Maryam said: 'O Allah, our Lord, send down on us a Table from out of heaven to be a festival for us, for the first of us and the last of us, and a sign from You. Provide for us. You are the best of providers.'

Allah said: 'I will send it down on you. Whoever of you disbelieves afterwards, I will punish him with such a punishment that I will not punish any other being.' (5: 112–15)

The Jews try to get rid of the Prophet 'Isa

The patience of the Jews ran out as their enmity and obstinacy increased. They wanted to be rid of 'Isa. They took his case to the Roman governor, saying: 'He is an anarchist, a revolutionary who has renounced our religion. He seduces our young men so they are led astray by him. He divides us, calls our dreams foolish and worries us.'

The style of avengers and politicians

The Jews said of 'Isa: 'He is a danger to the state. He does not submit to the government or obey the law. He does not respect the great nor revere the ancient. He is a revolutionary. If his evil is not contained, things will reach a crisis. Do not ignore a spark, no matter how trifling.'

Deceit and cunning

The Jews' words were full of deceit and cunning. They knew that mention of 'Isa's activities would not influence the governors nor provoke them, as their policy was not to meddle in the religious affairs of the Jews. That is why the Jews accused 'Isa of being involved in politics.

A problem

It was difficult for the Roman, idol-worshipping governors to decide on the truth of the matter and to recognize the motives of the Jews, and the reason for their enmity towards the Messiah. They were distracted from this question by administrative matters. But the Jews were very insistent and kept coming back to them. The Roman governors wanted to be finished with this case which had become the talk of the town.

The Prophet 'Isa in court

It was a Friday afternoon, before the night of the Sabbath. The Jews did not do anything on the Sabbath. It was a day of rest. They were very eager for the governors' judgement against 'Isa to be given before the sun set on Friday. Then they could go to sleep with peace of mind. They would be able to relax in the morning, with nothing to annoy them.

The judge was bored with the case. He had no interest in it nor did it contain any benefit for the Romans. The Jews gathered to hear the sentence. Time was short, the sun was nearly setting. The judge gave judgement against 'Isa, that he should be put to death by crucifixion.

The law at that time

The law at that time demanded that the condemned man be made to carry the cross on which he was to be crucified. The place of execution was a long way off. A crowd gathered, pushing against each other. The soldiers had no interest in the case. The Israelites all looked alike to them, they could not distinguish one from the other. It was evening and the shadows had lengthened. Some of the Jews and zealous fools among the young men were making fun of the Messiah. They were pushing him, cursing him, insulting him, keen to injure and humiliate him.

'Isa endures the injury

The Messiah was weary, exhausted by the effort and the length of time he had to stand in the court and the injuries he had to endure. The cross he carried was heavy. He could only go slowly.

Divine management

Then the soldier in charge of the procession commanded a young Israelite, who was the most zealous, the most foolish, the one most eager to injure and attack the Messiah, to carry the cross. The soldier wanted the whole business speedily resolved, to be free of the burdensome responsibility.

But it was a likeness of him

When the procession reached the place of execution, the gallows guard came forward to take charge of the condemned man from the city guard. They saw the young man carrying the cross. In the confusion, with the young men pushing and shouting, they seized hold of the man carrying the cross, thinking that he was the one condemned to be crucified. He was yelling and shouting, declaring that he was innocent and had nothing to do with the sentence. He had been made to carry the cross by force. The Roman soldiers paid no attention to him. They did not understand his dialect.

Carrying out the sentence

Every criminal claims that he is innocent of his crime. Every criminal shouts and cries out. The guards seized the young Israelite and carried out the sentence. The Jews were standing at a distance. Night was falling and everything was in darkness. They all thought that the crucified man was the Messiah.

'Isa was raised to heaven

As for the Prophet 'Isa, the son of Maryam, Allah the Exalted saved him from the plots of the Jews and raised him up to Himself, honoured him and purified him of those who had rejected.

The Qur'an recounts the story

These are Allah's words about the Jews:
'For their disbelief and uttering great slander against Maryam and their saying, "We killed the Messiah 'Isa son of Maryam, the Messenger of Allah." But they did not kill him nor crucify him, but only a likeness of that was shown to them. Those who disagreed about him are in doubt about him. They have no knowledge about him, only following conjectures. They did not truly kill him. Allah raised him to Himself. Allah is Mighty, the Wise.' (4:156)

He is in the heavens as Allah the Exalted, Who has the power to do anything He wills, willed him to be. His birth was a marvel, as were his life and everything about him. From first to last, he was a marvel, a miracle to confirm absolute Divine Power.

The descent of 'Isa before the Day of Resurrection

'Isa will descend from heaven when Allah wills. He will establish the proof against those of the Jews and Christians who abandoned him or went to excess about him. He will assist the truth and vanquish the people of falsehood, as our Prophet, may Allah bless him and grant him peace, has informed us. There are many sound reports and *ahadith* about this matter. The Muslims of every age believe in it. Allah the Sublime spoke this truth:

'There is not one of the People of the Book who will not believe in him before his death and on the Day of Rising he will be a witness against them.' (4: 159)

His good news about the sending of the Prophet Muhammad, may Allah bless him and grant him peace

'Isa did not complete his prophetic task due to the intense hostility and plotting of the Jews against him, and his own weakness and lack of helpers. He took leave of the people and obeyed his Lord's command. He gave them the good news of a Messenger to come after him whose job was to complete what he had begun. That message would spread throughout the world. Through him the blessing of Allah to His slaves would be completed and the proof against His creation established.

When 'Isa the son of Maryam said: 'O Children of Israel! I am the Messenger of Allah to you, confirming what is before me of the Torah and giving good news of a Messenger who will come after me whose name is Ahmad.' (61: 6)

From pure *Tawhid* to an obscure belief

One of the oddities in the history of religions makes one weep and one's heart bleed. It is that the Messiah's declaration of Allah's unity and his call to a clear religion, to worship Allah alone, seeking refuge in Him and having pure love for Him, was changed to an obscure creed and complicated philosophy.

Instead, his followers said: 'The Messiah is the son of Allah.' They said: 'Allah has taken a son.' They said: 'Allah is the Messiah, the son of Maryam.' They tried to make of the One Eternal God, who does not beget and

164

was not begotten, a family composed of three persons, all of them divine. They said: 'The father, the son and the Holy Ghost.'

They believe in Maryam, the mother of the Messiah, and elevate her to the level of sanctification and worship. They say: 'The Mother of God,' and statues and images of her are common in churches. The Christians bow to these images, seek refuge in them, and make supplication, vows and acts of devotion to them. Allah the Exalted has rejected such belief and worship:

The Messiah son of Maryam was only a Messenger. Messengers have passed away before him. His mother was a truthful woman. They both ate food. See how We make the signs clear to them. Then see how they have turned aside from the truth. Say: 'Do you worship, apart from Allah, what can neither hurt nor benefit you? Allah is the Hearing, the Knowing.' (5: 75–6)

'Isa calls to the worship of the One God

Like other Prophets, 'Isa called to the worship of the One God. His words have come in the Gospel: 'It is written that you prostrate to the Lord your God and worship Him alone.' (Matthew 4: 10); and: 'It is written that you prostrate to the Lord your God and worship Him alone.' (Luke 4: 8)

Allah the Exalted said: *'It is not fitting for any mortal to be given the Book, Judgement and Prophethood by Allah, and then for him to say to the people: "Be my slaves rather than Allah's." Rather: "Be faithful servants of God on account of what you know of the Book and what you study." He would not command you to take the angels and Prophets as Lords. Would he command you to unbelieve after you have surrendered?'* (3: 79–80)

The Qur'an clearly declares 'Isa's call

The Qur'an comprehends and confirms what was before it, and relates the clear statement of 'Isa about pure *tawhid* and his calling to it in clear, plain language:

They certainly disbelieve who say, 'God is the Messiah, the son of Maryam.' The Messiah said: 'O Children of Israel, worship Allah, my Lord and your Lord. Whoever associates anything with Allah, Allah will forbid him entrance to the Garden. His refuge is the Fire. The wrong-doers will have no helpers.' (5: 172)

The position of *Tawhid* in his call

'Isa said with a beautiful eloquence, relished by all who recognize the necessity of *tawhid and* the life of the Prophets and Messengers:

'The Messiah will not disdain to be a slave to Allah, neither the angels who are near to Him. Whoever disdains to worship Him and is arrogant, He will gather them to Him, all of them. As for those who believe and do righteous actions, He will pay them their wages in full and give them more from His bounty. As for those who disdain and are proud, He will punish them with a painful punishment. They will find no friend or helper apart from Allah.' (4: 172–3)

An awesome encounter in the gathering on the Day of Resurrection

The Qur'an, with its inimitable eloquence, depicts an awesome meeting on the Day of Resurrection. The

Prophet 'Isa will declare himself innocent of what the people said about him and of how they treated him. He will clarify his call with strength and truth, and pronounce the guilt of those of his community who went beyond the limits. They alone are responsible for this sin. Read the Qur'an and perceive how grand and majestic the situation would be, how splendid the scene: *When Allah said: "Isa the son of Maryam! Did you say to people, "Take me and my mother as gods apart from Allah"?' He said: "Glory be to Allah! It is not for me to say what I have no right to say. If I said it, You know it. You know what is in my soul and I do not know what is in Your soul. You know the unseen things. I only told them what You commanded me, 'Serve Allah, my Lord and your Lord.' I was a witness over them as long as I was among them. When You took me to You, You were the Watcher over them, and You are a witness of everything. If You punish them, they are Your slaves. If You forgive them, You are the Mighty, the Wise."'*

Allah said: 'This is the day when the truthful will profit by their truthfulness. They will have Gardens with rivers flowing under them, forever in them. Allah is pleased with them and they are pleased with Him. That is the great victory.'

To Allah belongs the kingdom of the heavens and the earth and what is in them. He has power over everything. (5: 116–20)

From an obscure creed to unveiled idolatry

It was on their own initiative that Christian missionaries moved to Europe: the Messiah never commanded that; he clearly stated that his mission was for the stray sheep, who were the erring men and women of the Israelites. In Europe at that time idol-worship was widespread. The Greeks were idol-worshippers. They made images of Allah in various forms, carved statues of those images, and built for them temples and shrines. There was a god for livelihood, a god for mercy and a god for power, and so on.

The Romans were deep-rooted in idol-worship and clung to superstition. Idolatry flowed through them like blood. When Christianity reached them and Constantine the Great became a Christian, embracing and adopting the new faith in 306 C.E., he made it the official state religion. Then Christianity began gradually to adopt many of the idolatrous beliefs found in Roman customs and Greek philosophy and to lose its prophetic purity, Eastern simplicity and unitarian zeal. Hypocrites entered it and grafted on to it their ancient beliefs and idolatrous ways. A new religion grew up in which Christianity and idol-worship mingled together.

So the early advance of Christianity was on a path other than the path followed by the Messiah and the one to which he called. It was like a traveller following a path deviating from the right one, intentionally or unintentionally, in the darkness of the night. He continues his journey on a path which is completely different from the original path.

The precise story is only known by those who study the history of this religion. Allah described the Christians as misguided, whereas He described the Jews as deserving of His wrath. He says on the tongue of the Muslims:

Guide us on the Straight Path, the path of those You have blessed, not those against whom You are angry nor those who are astray. (1: 7)

Allah's is the command first and last. (30: 4)

168

WORKBOOK

Questions on *Stories of the Prophets*

1. The Prophet Nuh

1. Why is the whole of mankind called the Children of Adam?

2. Why did Satan want to spoil a perfect world?

3. What methods did Satan consider using to draw people away from Allah?

4. Satan put into people's minds the idea of making portraits of dead people. What was the evil result of this action?

5. Describe the way in which foolish people used their idols.

6. Why was Allah angered by the worship of idols?

7. Describe Allah's angels.

8. Why did Allah prefer His messenger to be a man, rather than an angel?

9. Why was Nuh chosen to be a Prophet?

10. What did the foolish people say about Nuh being a Prophet?

169

11. Using Allah's words from the Holy Qur'an repeat how Nuh warned the idol-worshippers of their future punishment.

12. How did the rich people react to Nuh's warnings?

13. Name the signs of Allah that Nuh pointed out to the idol-worshippers.

14. For how many years was Nuh with his people?

15. Why is Nuh described as a patient Prophet?

16. Why did Nuh eventually appeal to Allah to punish his people?

17. How did Allah answer Nuh's plea?

18. Why did the people mock Nuh when he was building the ark?

19. What did Allah reveal should be saved on the ark?

20. Why was Nuh's son not saved? What important message is contained in the story of Nuh's son?

2. The Prophet Hud

1. From whom was the community of the 'Ad descended?

2. Describe the 'Ad's early, peaceful way of life.

3. Describe the changes in the 'Ad's behaviour once they forgot that they owed their blessings to Allah.

4. What differences appeared between the behaviour of the rich and of the poor as time went on?

5. Describe how Hud appealed to the people to improve their behaviour.

6. How did the 'Ad react to Hud's message from Allah?

7. Pick out the arguments that were used by both sides to justify their behaviour.

8. From the reasons given by Hud for worshipping Allah, pick out the one which you think makes the strongest case.

9. How did Allah punish the 'Ad?

10. Describe the scene of destruction witnessed by Hud and the believers.

3. The Prophet Salih

1. Who were the people of Thamud?

2. Describe the environment with which Allah had blessed the people of Thamud.

3. Why did the people of Thamud think that they could survive although the 'Ad had been destroyed?

4. Why did the people of Thamud need a Messenger from Allah?

5. Describe Salih's character.

6. Why did the rich people resist the message that Salih gave them from Allah?

7. Why did the rich people demand a sign to prove that Salih was telling the truth?

8. In your own words tell the story of the she-camel.

9. Why did the Thamud decide to kill this special she-camel and then to kill Salih?

10. How did Allah punish the wicked people of Thamud?

4. The Prophet Ibrahim

1. Why was Azar so well known?

2. Why did Ibrahim question why the people were worshipping idols?

3. Why did Azar get angry from hearing Ibrahim's questions?

4. Describe how Ibrahim proved to the people that idols are worthless.

5. How did the people react to Ibrahim's destruction of the idols?

6. How was Ibrahim saved from the fire?

7. Describe how Ibrahim convinced himself that Allah is greater than the stars, the moon and the sun.

8. What happened when Ibrahim gave the people the message from Allah?

9. Why was the king so angry when he discovered that Ibrahim worshipped Allah?

10. How did Ibrahim demonstrate to the king the greatness of Allah?

11. Why did Ibrahim decide to travel to another country?

12. Describe how Makka looked when Ibrahim and Hajar arrived there.

13. Describe how the well of Zamzam came into being.

14. Describe how Ibrahim's obedience to Allah was tested. How is the result of the feast celebrated each year?

15. Find a picture of the Al-Aqsa mosque in Jerusalem. Describe how it was first built.

5. The Prophet Yusuf

1. Ibrahim had a son named Ishaq and Ishaq had a son named Ya'qub. Ya'qub had 12 sons including one named Yusuf. What was the relationship between the Prophet Yusuf and the Prophet Ibrahim?

2. Relate the story of Yusuf's wonderful dream and then give his father's interpretation of this dream.

3. Why were the other brothers jealous of Yusuf and Benyamin?

4. By what means did the brothers persuade their father to let Yusuf go away with them?

5. How did the brothers get rid of Yusuf and how did they explain his absence to their father?

6. Describe how Yusuf was rescued from the well.

7. Who bought Yusuf and to whom was he given?

8. Describe the dreams Yusuf's fellow prisoners had and his interpretation of their dreams.

9. Why was Yusuf summoned from the prison to the king's palace?

10. What was the warning Yusuf gave to the king about Egypt's food supplies?

11. Why did Yusuf's brothers travel to Egypt?

12. How did Yusuf persuade his brothers to bring Benyamin to Egypt?

13. How did Yusuf persuade his brothers to leave Benyamin with him in Egypt?

14. When the brothers went to Egypt for the third time they discovered Yusuf's true identity. How did they make this discovery?

15. Describe the scene when Ya'qub learnt that Yusuf was still alive and explain how Yusuf's original dream had come true.

6. The Prophet Musa

1. Why did the Egyptians start to lose their respect for the Israelites?

2. How did the Pharaohs treat the Israelites?

3. Why did the Israelites refuse to worship the Pharaoh?

4. Why did the Pharaoh order that all the new born baby boys of the Israelites be put to death?

5. Describe how the baby Musa was saved.

6. What injustices did Musa notice when he was growing up in the palace?

7. Why did the Pharaoh order that Musa be put to death?

8. How did Allah help Musa to escape from the Pharaoh's orders?

9. Describe how Musa was provided with a home in Midian for eight years.

10. With what words did Allah speak to Musa when he and his family left the house in Midian?

11. What two signs did Allah give to Musa before commanding him to return to Egypt?

12. Why was it best for Musa and Harun to be kind to the Pharaoh at first?

13. What arguments did Musa use to convince the Pharaoh that there is only one God?

14. What happened when the king summoned all the best sorcerers to use their magic against Musa?

15. What convinced the sorcerers that Musa was a Prophet?

16. How did the sorcerers react to the Pharaoh's threats when they were accused of betraying him?

17. What advice did the wise believer give to the Pharaoh?

18. Why was the Pharaoh's wife a brave woman?

19. By what means did Allah make the Pharaoh take notice of Him?

20. Name the five signs Allah sent to the Pharaoh.

21. Describe how Musa led the Israelites out of Egypt.

22. What happened to the Pharaoh and his armies when he pursued the Israelites?

23. How were the Israelites helped when they were hungry and thirsty in the desert?

24. Why did the Israelites behave like spoilt children after they left Egypt?

25. Relate the story of how a murderer was caught with Allah's help.

26. Give five reasons why the *Shari'ah* is necessary.

27. In what way did Allah provide the Israelites with guidance on Mount Sinai?

28. How did the Samiri lead the weak Israelites astray?

29. Describe the meeting between Musa and Al-Khadir and explain why it enabled Musa to understand how Allah has distributed knowledge.

30. The Prophet Musa rescued the Israelites from the Pharaoh and led them to freedom. Describe the behaviour of the Israelites after they were rescued and how Allah punished them.

7. The Prophet Shu'ayb

1. Why was Shu'ayb's message from Allah needed by Midian and the people of the Thicket?

2. Give three of Shu'ayb's reasons for being fair in business dealings.

3. Describe how Shu'ayb's people ignored his advice.

4. What was the people's final threat to Shu'ayb?

5. How did Allah punish the wicked people who rejected Shu'ayb's advice?

8. The Prophets Da'ud and Sulayman

1. What does the Holy Qur'an say about the Prophets Sulayman and Da'ud (ref. 27: 16, 34: 10, 21: 79–80).

2. Describe how Da'ud ruled his kingdom.

3. What was Sulayman's wise judgement in the case where sheep had ruined a man's vineyard?

4. Find a picture of the bird called a hoopoe. How did the hoopoe help Sulayman?

5. What did the Queen of Sheba and her people worship?

6. Why did Sulayman write a letter to the Queen of Sheba?

7. How did the Queen's counsellors respond to the letter?

8. What did the Queen decide to send to Sulayman and what were her reasons for sending them?

9. How did Sulayman react to the Queen's test?

10. Why did Sulayman decide to send for the Queen's throne?

11. Describe how the Queen was to be tested about her own throne.

12. Why did Sulayman want to test the Queen's powers of perception?

13. How did Sulayman discover that the Queen of Sheba was easily deceived?

14. What did the Queen say when she realized that she lacked perception?

15. How does this story illustrate Sulayman's wisdom?

9. The Prophets Ayyub and Yunus

1. Describe the harsh conditions endured by Ayyub and his wife.

2. How did Ayyub's patience show up?

3. What does the Holy Qur'an say about Ayyub's prayer to Allah and Allah's answer?

4. To which village did Allah send Yunus and why did Allah send him there?

5. Describe Yunus' experiences from the time he embarked on the ship until Allah answered his prayer.

10. The Prophets Zakariyya and Yahya

1. How was old Zakariyya's prayer answered?

2. What did Imran's wife (a relative of Zakariyya's) vow that she would do if she had a son?

3. 'Imran's wife had a daughter, not a son. Why was this daughter entrusted to Zakariyya's care?

4. Describe the character of Yahya, the son of Zakariyya.

5. Relate what the Holy Qur'an says about Yahya in 19: 12–15.

11. The Prophet 'Isa ibn Maryam

1. Why was 'Isa's birth a miracle?

2. Describe the condition of the Jews at the time of 'Isa's birth.

3. Name five of 'Isa's good qualities.

4. Describe five of the miracles 'Isa performed.

5. Why did the Jews find it difficult to accept the message 'Isa gave them from Allah?

6. Why did 'Isa devote his teaching to the poor and not to the rich?

7. Why was it wrong for 'Isa's disciples to want him to ask Allah to send down a table?

8. How did Allah reply to the disciples' request?

9. Why did the Jews want to be rid of 'Isa?

10. Why did the Roman governor want to be rid of 'Isa's case?

11. Describe the scene when 'Isa was marched towards the execution site.

12. What happened when the procession reached the execution site?

13. From the Holy Qur'an repeat Allah's words about 'Isa's death (4: 156).

14. Read what the Holy Qur'an says about 'Isa (5: 75–6). How does this contradict Christian belief?

15. How did 'Isa's message from Allah become distorted?